# CONTENTS

Fleet in Focus: Bibby's four masters Part 2 *Mark Bedford* — 2

Whitbury Shipping Co. Ltd. *Ken Garrett* — 14

Two-funnel tankers *David Burrell* — 22

Port Line's golden era *Peter Newall* — 26

Torquay harbour in the thirties Part 1 *David Eeles* — 30

POLSKAROB *Jerzy Swieszkowski and Bohdan Huras* — 37

*Dominic* and her Brazilian crew *Captain A.W. Kinghorn* — 48

The British C1-M-AV1s — 54

Putting Burns and Laird straight — 57

Sources and acknowledgements — 58

Putting the Record straight — 59

## Ships in Focus Publications

*Correspondence and editorial:*
Roy Fenton
18 Durrington Avenue
London SW20 8NT
020 8879 3527
rfenton@rfenton.demon.co.uk

*Orders and photographic:*
John & Marion Clarkson
18 Franklands, Longton
Preston PR4 5PD
01772 612855
sales@shipsinfocus.co.uk

Printed by Amadeus Press Ltd., Cleckheaton.

Designed by Hugh Smallwood, John Clarkson and Roy Fenton.

SHIPS IN FOCUS RECORD

ISBN 1 901703 10 X

# SHIPS IN FOCU

CW00322036

The editors have been puzzling shipping company histories which but too short to make up a book *British Shipping Fleets*, a hardback book which brings together the histories and fleet lists of a number of medium-sized companies. Each is compiled to the same standards we aim for in *Record*, so that they are thoroughly-researched yet readable, and include well reproduced photographs of as many ships as possible. The company histories cover a broad spread: a 20th century liner and container company, a steam coaster owner, a Cardiff tramp company, a specialist newsprint carrier, and an old-established east coast Scottish liner company. As well as telling the story of these companies, features elaborate on aspects of maritime history which arise in the text. We believe *British Shipping Fleets* will appeal to those who read *Record*, and so we will be offering copies to subscribers post-free: watch for details. Publication of *British Shipping Fleets* does not mean that *Record* will not be carrying company histories in future; indeed, this issue includes two.

We have taken the opportunity of beginning what we regard, nominally, as the fourth volume of *Record* to make subtle changes to our typographic design. The most noticeable is that ships' names in the text will appear in upper and lower case italics, a change we have made to improve readability.

As we announced in the editorial for issue 12, this *Record* is the first published at a shorter frequency. Approximately three-months is probably the 'natural' interval between issues of a journal such as ours, which does not carry news, but which does seek to publish readers' comments and feedback on articles as soon as possible. Expect *Record* 14 early in December.

John Clarkson                             Roy Fenton

July 2000

## SUBSCRIPTION RATES FOR RECORD

Subscribers make a saving on the postage of three issues, and receive each *Record* just as soon as it is published. They are also eligible for concessions on newly-published *Ships in Focus* titles. Readers can start their subscription with *any* issue, and are welcome to backdate it to receive previous issues.

| | |
|---|---|
| UK | £23 |
| Europe (airmail) | £25 |
| Rest of world (surface mail) | £25 |
| Rest of world (airmail) | £30 |

*Gloucestershire* see page 2

## Fleet in Focus
# BIBBY'S FOUR-MASTERS Part 2
## Mark Bedford

**GLOUCESTERSHIRE** (above)
*Harland and Wolff Ltd., Belfast; 1910, 8,124gt, 482 feet*
*Two Q. 4-cyl. by Harland and Wolff Ltd., Belfast; 823 NHP driving twin screws*
*Gloucestershire*, sistership to *Leicestershire* (see *Record* 12, page 201), was delivered on 22nd October 1910 and replaced *Cheshire* of 1891.

In August 1914 *Gloucestershire* was requisitioned to carry troops and horses to France and to return as an ambulance transport. She was taken over by the Royal Navy in December 1915 and, converted into the armed merchant cruiser (AMC) HMS *Gloucestershire*, saw service with Atlantic convoys. Later she joined the 10th Cruiser Squadron for North Sea patrol work, but in 1917 was converted back into a troopship.

After returning to her builders in 1919 for a full refit and conversion to oil-firing, *Gloucestershire* went back to the Burma service until replaced by the *Derbyshire* in early 1936. The old ship was sold for scrap to T.W. Ward Ltd. arriving at Pembroke Dock on 2nd February.

**OXFORDSHIRE** (opposite page)
*Harland and Wolff Ltd., Belfast; 1912, 8,624gt, 494 feet*
*Two Q. 4-cyl. by Harland and Wolff Ltd., Belfast; 906 NHP driving twin screws*
*Oxfordshire*, delivered on 17th September 1912, was an enlarged version of *Gloucestershire* with a longer boat deck and housing, but also differed from the latter in having her small bunker hatch forward of the funnel replaced by coaling ports. The after section of her bridge deck was open on the starboard side only for about 45 feet, a feature seen also on *Leicestershire*, *Gloucestershire* and the later *Lancashire*, and possibly designed to help ventilation on the outward passage.

*Oxfordshire* was the first merchant ship to be requisitioned in 1914, two days before Britain's declaration of war. She was converted into a hospital ship for the Royal Navy but they found her too large so she switched to the Army for cross-Channel work, followed by service in the Dardanelles. More cross-Channel work was followed by service in the Salonica campaign from October 1915 onwards, Mesopotamia, and East Africa from December 1916. On 24th March 1918 she paid off and returned to Bibbys who operated her under the Liner Requisition Scheme until the end of the war. In 1919 she was refitted and converted to oil-burning by her builders. The upper

photograph opposite shows her in Barry during the First World War.

*Oxfordshire* spent all the inter-war period on Bibby's Burma route but in 1939 was called up for war service again. From November 1939 she went to Freetown, Sierra Leone as a hospital ship until returning home for a refit in September 1942. She was at the North Africa landings, Operation Torch, in November 1942 and remained in the Mediterranean until 1944. After sustaining damage following a near miss from an aerial bomb on 29th October 1944 in the Adriatic she went to Australia to prepare for service with the British Pacific fleet. She was loaned to the US Navy for the invasion of Okinawa in April 1945, and was present at the liberation of Hong Kong in September, and then served with the Red Cross in the Far East, Mediterranean and the North Atlantic until 19th July 1948.

Later in 1948 *Oxfordshire* sailed on one charter voyage to Jeddah with pilgrims before being refitted and converted to an emigrant ship. From April 1949 until October she sailed with emigrants to Australia and afterwards worked again as a troopship until February 1951 when she was withdrawn from service and put up for sale. The following month she was sold to

the Pan-Islamic Steamship Co. of Karachi for the pilgrim service and for running between Karachi and the East Pakistan port of Chittagong. Renamed *Safina-e-Arab* she could carry 101 first-class, 46 second-class, and 1,085 third-class passengers.

Her end came after she was laid up in November 1957 and sold for scrap at Karachi in April 1958. As *Safina-e-Arab*, she was featured on page 60 of *Record* 9, in Peter Newall's feature on pilgrim ships.

*Oxfordshire*, the last Bibby vessel to retain her four masts, carried more casualties in either World War than any other hospital ship. *[Top: National Maritime Museum P38728]*

## LANCASHIRE (2)
*Harland and Wolff Ltd., Belfast; 1917, 9,445gt, 501 feet*
*Two Q. 4-cyl. by Harland and Wolff Ltd., Belfast; 942 NHP driving twin screws*

The second *Lancashire* was the first Bibby ship to have a cruiser stern, but this was possibly a war-time modification. She was ordered in 1913 and laid down in 1914 for delivery in 1915, but work stopped in August 1914 with the outbreak of war. Work was resumed two years later following heavy merchant shipping losses and she

was delivered on 9th August 1917 to go straight on to the Burma service under the Liner Requisition Scheme. She could carry 295 first class passengers, and had the same engines as *Oxfordshire* although her boilers were fractionally larger giving 942 compared with 906 NHP. Completed as a coal burner, her bunker capacity was 1,020 tons.

After the Armistice *Lancashire* went onto repatriation work, first for the French and Belgians and later for the Australians and Americans, until released in

1920. After refitting and conversion to oil-firing she re-entered Bibby's service, and then in 1930 was chosen to become a full-time troopship. She was converted by Cammell Laird, Birkenhead to carry 1,200 troops, and 320 officers and family members and given troopship livery but she kept her four-mast rig. Both well decks were filled in, her boat deck was extended to the stern, extra lifeboats were fitted, and her draught reduced by more than four feet. Together with the motorships *Dorsetshire* and *Somersetshire*, *Lancashire* trooped to

4

the Far East, Near East and India, spending slack periods laid up in the River Dart. With the outbreak of the Second World War, the pace of trooping inevitably increased and at the Normandy Landings *Lancashire* was commodore ship of a column of four Bibby troopships. Later converted into a depot and repair ship for the Far East she arrived too late to see much service, and after VJ Day went to Hong Kong to do restoration work.

In 1946 *Lancashire* was converted back to a trooper at Harland and Wolff's Govan yard. Her main mast was removed, further extensions made to her superstructure aft and shortly afterwards three after lifeboats on each side were replaced by one motorboat per side. She trooped continuously until February 1956 when she was sold for scrap, arriving at Barrow-in-Furness on 6th April. Three of the accompanying photographs show Lancashire in her post-war condition, the upper one on this page being dated 6th August 1947. *[Opposite bottom: National Maritime Museum P23185]*

**YORKSHIRE (2)** (top and bottom this page)
*Harland and Wolff Ltd., Belfast; 1920, 10,148gt, 501 feet*
*Four steam turbines by Harland and Wolff Ltd., Belfast; 946 NHP 5,500 SHP driving twin screws*

Ordered in 1918 and launched on 29th May 1919, shortages and strikes delayed the second *Yorkshire's* delivery until 2nd September 1920. The *Yorkshire* had a distinctive position in the fleet: she was the only four-master to be built flush-decked which gave her a particularly fine appearance; she was the last steam-driven four-master; the only one to have geared turbines; and the last to be fitted with a really tall funnel. Thanks to the extra high engine-room casing her funnel stood 70 feet above the boat deck. Her passenger capacity of 303 first-class was reduced to 287 in the 1930s, and her crew numbered about 190.

The same length as *Lancashire* but one foot wider at the beam, and with similar boilers and turbines, *Yorkshire* developed 5,500 SHP at her service speed of 15 knots, with a maximum of 6,500 SHP. But *Yorkshire* was unlucky in suffering continual machinery problems including overheating and high fuel consumption. She was built at a time when gearing was just being introduced to steam turbines, and the cutting of gear wheels was a skill yet to be perfected. Around 1927 her gearbox installation was completely rebuilt and this seems to have resolved her mechanical problems. In the early 1930s the forward end of the boat was plated in for about 25 feet on each side with the inclusion of five large windows (lower photograph).

In 1925 whilst navigating the Elbe in fog she was collision with the Chargeurs Reunis liner *Groix*, which had to be beached. Disaster came for *Yorkshire* on

17th October 1939 when, as commodore ship of a convoy and carrying 118 passengers, she was hit by two torpedoes from U 37 about 250 miles north west of Cape Finisterre. Sinking in about nine minutes with the loss of 33 passengers and 25 crew, she was the second passenger ship loss of the war.

**SHROPSHIRE (2)** (opposite)
*Fairfield Shipbuilding and Engineering Co. Ltd., Govan; 1926, 10,560gt, 502 feet*
*Two 8-cyl. 2SCSA Sulzer oil engines by Fairfield Shipbuilding and Engineering Co. Ltd., Govan; 2,196 NHP, 7,700 BHP driving twin screws*

*Shropshire* was the first ship for Bibby's Burma service that was not built by Harland and Wolff, essentially because their Burmeister and Wain-type engine was too tall to fit the Belfast builder's plan for these passenger ships. The contract went instead to Fairfields, who were licensed to fit compact Swiss Sulzer engines, the result being that the next six 'Burma' ships plus one Bibby troopship were built on the Clyde.

*Shropshire's* service speed was the standard 15 to 15.5 knots and her daily fuel consumption was about 22 tons. She had *Lancashire's* well deck arrangement but with a built-up-amidships superstructure, and the small midships hatch just forward of the funnel (the old bunker hatch) which had made its comeback on the *Yorkshire*.

The funnel was shorter and slightly thicker than before but was well proportioned - and still a typical Bibby steamship funnel on a motorship. She had a passenger capacity of 265 (later 275) and a crew of 200.

Shropshire gave very satisfactory service, and in the Second World War was soon requisitioned for conversion to an AMC, armed with six 6-inch, two 3-inch and some small AA guns. In October 1939 she was commissioned as HMS Salopian because there was already a heavy cruiser named HMS Shropshire. The lower photograph shows her in Number 3 Dry Dock in the West Float, Birkenhead in September 1940, probably undergoing the refit that left her with only her foremast and the stump of the jigger mast. HMS Salopian was on convoy and patrol work from October 1939 until sunk by U 98 off Greenland on 13th May 1941.

## CHESHIRE (2)

*Fairfield Shipbuilding and Engineering Co. Ltd., Govan; 1927, 10,552gt, 502 feet*

*Two 8-cyl. 2SCSA Sulzer oil engines by Fairfield Shipbuilding and Engineering Co. Ltd., Govan; 2,196 NHP, 7,700 BHP driving twin screws*

*Cheshire*, Bibby's second motorship, was launched in April 1927 and delivered in July to replace *Warwickshire* of 1902. She was to prove as trouble-free as her sister, *Shropshire*.

When war began *Cheshire* was sent to Calcutta for conversion to an AMC and fitted with guns like her sister. Commissioned on 30th October 1939, she proceeded to the UK before taking up convoy and escort duties. On 14th October 1940 she was torpedoed in the North Atlantic, and was towed back but had to be beached at Carrickfergus when approaching Belfast. Repairs took six months, but she was back in service until torpedoed again on 18th August 1942. After further repairs she

re-emerged as a troopship and took part in the Normandy landings together with her old fleet mates *Lancashire*, *Devonshire* and *Worcestershire*.

She is seen below on 24th September 1947, on the trooping and repatriation duties on which she remained until 5th October 1948. *Cheshire* was then selected to be an emigrant ship and returned to her builders for a refit and conversion to carry 650 passengers. She became flush-decked and extra lifeboats

and various extensions were fitted, although she retained her original funnel and foremast, as seen opposite and above. She joined the emigrant service in August 1949, which by the end of the year had grown to nine vessels. In February 1953 she was chartered for troopship service during the Korean War and was retained for such work until February 1957 when she was laid up. One of her last duties was to take stores and personnel to Christmas Island for the British nuclear bomb tests. She arrived at Newport, Monmouthshire for demolition by Cashmores on 11th July 1957. [*This page: Fotoflite incorporating Skyfotos*]

## STAFFORDSHIRE (2)

*Fairfield Shipbuilding and Engineering Co. Ltd., Govan; 1929, 10,654gt, 502 feet*
*Two 8-cyl. 2SCSA Sulzer oil engines by Fairfield Shipbuilding and Engineering Co. Ltd., Govan; 2,196 NHP, 7,700 BHP driving twin screws*

*Staffordshire* was ordered in 1927, soon after delivery of *Cheshire*, was launched in October 1928, delivered in January 1929 and sailed on her maiden voyage on 22nd February 1929. She was a repeat of *Cheshire* but with an increase in beam of nearly two feet, and she seems to have been as satisfactory as her predecessors. Like them she had the forward end of the boat deck enclosed on each side with large windows under the forward lifeboat. In the 1930s her four pairs of midships davits were replaced with a modern gravity type which allowed the boat deck to be cleared and enlarged. Her passenger capacity was 273 with a crew of 200.

Requisitioned as a troopship in April 1940, *Staffordshire* was attacked by enemy aircraft on 28th March 1941 when north west of Scotland. Fourteen passengers and 14 crew lost their lives when she was abandoned, but she was later re-boarded by the crew. She is seen opposite top in Loch Ewe on 29th April 1941 with alongside her the tug *Kings Cross* (1918/282) and the Dutch motor coaster *Nato* (399/1939). Repaired on the Tyne *Staffordshire* returned to service in January 1942 as a trooper for 1,800 men and saw action at the South of France landings (Anvil) in August 1944. After preparing for the Malaya landings (Zipper) in September

"STAFFORDSHIRE"

1945, *Staffordshire* was used for repatriation and trooping duties, and the lower photograph was probably taken at this time. Her last such voyage was with reinforcements to Singapore at the start of the Malayan Emergency.

Released to Bibby in November 1948, *Staffordshire* was the last pre-war ship to be refitted. She returned to her builders for a full refit and conversion to a passenger cargo ship with a capacity for 109 (later 113) passengers. Only her foremast and squat funnel remained. The superstructure was cut down aft, giving a long aft well deck for No. 5 and 6 hatches with two pairs of samson posts. This refit was completed in September 1949 and, though practical, the result was visually a disaster. *Staffordshire* was the first of the fleet to be retired: she completed her last round voyage on 4th July 1959, and on 25th July left Liverpool as *Stafford Maru* bound for Osaka to be scrapped. *[This page top: National Maritime Museum N37159]*

## WORCESTERSHIRE (2)

*Fairfield Shipbuilding and Engineering Co. Ltd., Govan; 1931, 11,453gt, 502 feet*

*Two 8-cyl. 2SCSA Sulzer oil engines by Fairfield Shipbuilding and Engineering Co. Ltd., Govan; 2,196 NHP, 7,700 BHP driving twin screws*

*Worcestershire*, Bibby's fourth motorship, was launched in October 1930 and completed on 5th February 1931. Although her beam was again increased while the main engines were unchanged in rating and power there is no evidence that she lacked power or speed. Her distinctive feature was the raising of the boat deck amidships by one deck to give a continuous deck with six boats on each side. Around 1937 new gravity davits were fitted, and the boats on the housing between the mizzen and jigger masts were removed. When the forward section of the promenade-deck was enclosed *Worcestershire* looked virtually identical with *Derbyshire*.

*Worcestershire* was requisitioned in November 1939 as an armed merchant cruiser, fitted with the usual six 6-inch guns plus some smaller ones, and served on convoy escort duties until torpedoed in the North Atlantic on 3rd April 1941. She reached Liverpool safely, but her repairs were not completed until December 1941. Further service followed in the Indian Ocean, but in June 1943 she was converted to a troopship for 2,000 personnel.

*Worcestershire* was at the Normandy landings and was due to take part in the Malaya landings in September 1945. Repatriation and troop work continued until her release from Government service in October 1947 by which time she had carried 80,000 men without accident. After returning to her builders for a full refit and conversion (very similar to that of the *Staffordshire*), she re-entered Bibby's Burma service in January 1949 with a passenger capacity of 115 (below). Her career ended in December 1961, when she arrived for breaking up at Osaka as the *Kannon Maru*. [Bottom: Fotoflite incorporating Skyfotos]

## DERBYSHIRE (2)

*Fairfield Shipbuilding and Engineering Co. Ltd., Govan; 1935, 11,660gt, 502 feet*
*Two 8-cyl. 2SCSA Sulzer oil engines by Fairfield Shipbuilding and Engineering Co. Ltd., Govan; 2,252 NHP, 8,000 BHP driving twin screws*

*Derbyshire* (2), which sailed on her maiden voyage on 5th November 1935, was the last ship to be built with the four-mast rig. Although trade was steadily improving by the end of 1935, the added cost of this must have been hard to justify. She was very similar to the *Worcestershire*, although her beam was two feet greater, and her main engines were uprated. Her passenger capacity was also increased to 292 first class with 224 crew. Bibby's fleet was at its peak in the late 1930s, and it is unlikely that a comparable fleet of such individual ships has operated anywhere in the last 50 years.

November 1939 saw *Derbyshire* commissioned as an armed merchant cruiser and, like Bibby's other vessels, conversion to carry guns left her with just the foremast and the stump of her jigger mast. She finished convoy escort and patrol duties in the north and western approaches in May 1942, and was then converted to a troopship. After taking part in the North Africa Landings in November 1942 she underwent another conversion to a landing ship infantry (large) and had five very large sets of davits fitted on both sides. She then carried 20 landing craft in pairs and saw service in the landings in Sicily, Anzio, and the south of France. From January 1945 she was in the Burma campaign and was the first Allied ship to enter Rangoon in May 1945. She became the headquarters ship for the re-occupation of Singapore in September 1945. Trooping and repatriation work continued until her release in November 1946. In the years between requisition and release *Derbyshire* had steamed 330,000 miles and carried 136,000 troops.

The first Bibby's ship to be released, she returned to her builders for a refit and conversion which was completed in November 1947. Like *Worcestershire* her gross tonnage was reduced as was her passenger capacity (from 291 to 115) and her speed (14 knots). She now had just two masts and a large funnel of modern motorship style (below). Her superstructure was shortened but because no alteration was made to her vertical stem she looked unbalanced. Nevertheless, *Derbyshire* was the best looking of the three pre-war ships as she alone kept her mainmast. She was outlived by one year by the post-war *Warwickshire* and *Leicestershire*, arriving at Hong Kong for breaking up on 18th February 1964. *[Bottom: Author's collection]*

# WHITBURY SHIPPING CO. LTD.
## Ken Garrett

Whitbury Shipping Co. Ltd. was formed in 1974 by the major shareholders, Trevor Jewsbury and Jack Whiting, the company name being based on a combination of their surnames. Trevor Jewsbury was a Trinity House Pilot and Jack Whiting, from a well known Medway barging family, had been a master with Crescent Shipping. He went ashore in 1970 but had returned to sea shortly afterwards in command of the *Jo* (400/1955). The ship was running between Brussels and Rochester with reinforcing bars and other steel products for M. Lynch and Sons Ltd. of Rochester.

Relief masters were very hard to find and Jack had been aboard for a couple of years unable to take any proper leave when, through a mutual friend, he contacted Trevor and persuaded him to relieve him for a month. Trevor enjoyed the experience and later, talking to Jack, discussed a mutual ambition to own and operate a small ship. Some while later Jack telephoned Trevor, reminding him of the conversation and asked if he was still of the same mind. Both remained keen and were able to raise about £5,000 each for the venture.

The partners understood ships from the practical point of view and knew the type they wanted. It had to be below 500 gross tons, in good repair, well maintained and not requiring any expensive surveys for a couple of years. Such a ship would certainly be priced well above their capital of £10,000 besides being difficult to find. Banks were singularly unhelpful but by a stroke of good luck they were put in contact with Concord Leasing Ltd. of

Brentford in Essex. Concord were involved in leasing vehicles, buses, tractors, had recently financed light aeroplanes and were keen to extend their activities to ships. Another stroke of luck took them to the *Borelly* (430/1956).

### Borelly

*Borelly's* owner-master, Captain Eltje Martin Hut, had laid the ship up for eighteen months in a canal near Delfzijl in the north of Holland and looked after her well. Normally he would take the ship into the Baltic each spring, just as the ice was melting, and load loose, sawn timber. Known in the trade as deals, battens and boards, it was consigned mainly to the smaller ports in Holland, Britain and Ireland. This work would continue until the loading ports froze over in the late autumn when Captain Hut would take his ship to Delfzijl for maintenance and repairs, doing much of the work himself. Naturally, the ship would carry other cargoes, but loose timber was the main activity. The nature of the timber trade was changing rapidly at the time and an ever increasing quantity was being bundled into packages before shipment. This method favoured larger ships where broken stowage was not such a problem and, where they lost out on volume, they made up in speed of turnround and reduction in handling costs. This effectively spelled the end of the loose timber trade and thus the traditional summer work of ships like the *Borelly*. Captain Hut, by this time 68 and not in the best of health, was not keen to go into general trading and laid up his ship while on medical advice he sought a buyer.

*Borelly* (1) whilst still under the Dutch flag *[C.A. Hill]*

The fact that the ship had been laid up for eighteen months and had an imminent special survey gave the partners some cause for concern. Their fears were allayed to some extent when enquiries revealed that the lay up was due to the owner rather than to the ship. They were also encouraged by the classification society, Bureau Veritas, who indicated that they would allow full time credit for the lay up period when granting an extension of class. A further cause for concern was that although the engine, including the sump, had been scrupulously cleaned they had not seen the engine running because Captain Hut was unwilling to spend money on lubricating oil and the subsequent cleaning merely for a buyers' inspection. However, everything else was in such an immaculate condition that they felt justified in taking the chance.

The *Borelly* was one of a number of similar ships, built for the Baltic loose timber trade where three gangs of stevedores would be employed to load them. Although not expected to navigate in ice of any real thickness, most had a basic ice classification. This meant that they were stiffened forward with thicker plates and had a specified minimum engine power. The benefits were that they were strong ships with a reserve of power that outweighed the penalties of slightly higher bunker consumption and a slightly reduced deadweight for the size of ship. Their strength and operating flexibility earned them an enviable reputation and their eclipse by more sophisticated and expensive replacements was viewed with dismay by many of the older continental shipmasters.

*Borelly* was purchased by Concord Leasing Ltd. in May 1974 with a three-year lease to Whitbury Shipping Ltd. This company would acquire the ship at the end of the leasing period, through a third party to satisfy the requirements of contemporary legislation. The handover at Delfzijl was not without incident as the Dutch bank apparently 'lost' the money transferred from London for a few days, thereby probably earning themselves some windfall interest. Trevor Jewsbury sailed on the ship as master with Captain Hut and his wife on board as supernumeraries. The ship carried the first Whitbury cargo when she loaded fertilizers at Sluiskil for discharge at Gunness before going on to Rochester where the change of flag surveys and other formalities were carried out.

Jack Whiting took the ship away from Rochester as master and was relieved occasionally by Trevor. Jack was accompanied by his wife, Jan, who took on the role of chief steward looking after the catering, stores and general housekeeping aboard.

During the inspections and subsequently, the ship had seemed too good to be true but Jack had always thought that there had to be a catch. His prophetic thoughts caught up with him when the main engine crankshaft seized as the ship arrived at Terneuzen. When the crankcase doors were opened for inspection white metal could be seen hanging down like icicles from the bottom ends. A local repair firm, thinking that they had a sitting duck, put in a ridiculous quote for the work and stipulated that they would need payment in full before the ship could sail. The situation was desperate: the ship had barely earned any money and the insurance claim was unlikely to be settled in time. In the end, a gang of fitters was brought across from England who carried out the repair for much less than the local quote and, as a bonus, Whitbury was given time to pay.

Five months later the same thing happened again. This time the ship was in the Medway and the repair was carried out by the Acorn Shipyard. The cause was found to be a misalignment of the intermediate shaft and the plummer bearings, probably as a result of a much earlier incident. All was put right and no more problems occurred on this account. *Borelly* had a good cubic capacity but suffered somewhat, particularly when offering for deadweight cargoes, by being unable to lift her full deadweight. Nevertheless, she proved herself to be reliable and a good money earner.

Apart from the usual run of coastal cargoes the ship was occasionally involved in something different. One charter was to carry materials, stores and equipment destined for North Sea oil rigs from Grangemouth to the Flotta Base in Scapa Flow. Another was to carry barrels of pickled herrings from the Isle of Man to the Wilhelminahaven in Rotterdam and return with empty barrels. The residual smell was anathema to most cargo inspectors and had to be disguised after the charter before loading even the least sensitive commodities.

**Whitbury's organisation**

The partners had decided that since they had neither the time nor the expertise to carry out their own chartering, they would offer the ship to one of the professional freight managers. The well-known London-based company, Temple, Thompson and Clark, was chosen. In such arrangements the manager finds the cargoes, negotiates the freight rates and charter party clauses, and finally collects the freight earnings when the voyage has been completed. He probably pays some commission to the shipper and his broker, pays the port costs, agency fees, stevedoring, pilotage and boatmen, concludes all the post fixture work, takes out his own commission and pays the balance, or net freight as it is known, to the owner. Out of this net freight the owner has to pay all the other expenses. These include insurance, bunkers, stores, wages, surveys, repairs, spare parts and all the other items necessary to run a ship. Even if an owner runs his ship efficiently and economically, he is still in the hands of his freight manager to obtain good paying cargoes without lengthy ballast passages in between, to play his part in keeping the port expenses to a minimum and, above all, to pay the balance of the freight money promptly. The relationship between a shipowner and his freight manager is a delicate affair requiring a considerable degree of trust. It is inevitable that some misunderstandings will arise, particularly in the level of freight rates and address commissions.

After about four years' trading, Whitbury Shipping decided to think again. They considered employing their own chartering manager but decided against it and transferred their business to Halcyon Shipping Ltd. of Great Yarmouth who were to remain the company's freight managers until all the ships were sold. For the most part, the ships were engaged on voyages between Britain and the near continent carrying grain, steel, fertilizers, coal and other common commodities.

From the start, the partners agreed on an economic operation with as few frills as possible. One manifestation of this was the retention of the ships' original names except in the case of the two former Weston Shipping vessels, where the purchase agreement insisted upon a change of name. The foreign-flag ships were brought under the British flag and registered in Rochester with the least possible expense. There had been some discussions in the early days about a standard colour scheme, funnel mark and house flag for the ships. This was never really resolved although there was a predilection for grey hulls, later changing to blue, with a white superstructure. A blue funnel with a white band was also the preferred scheme and, in the early days, the letters WS appeared on the white band. There were variations depending on the artistic ability of the crew and their enthusiasms. The matter was not pressed because, as the ships ostensibly traded as part of the freight manager's fleet rather than as Whitbury Shipping, it was thought that to raise the company profile by adopting an identifiable house style would be unlikely to bestow any commercial advantage.

To keep costs down, the partners sought cheap sources of supply of paint and other stores, inevitably meaning that they had to make do with what they could get and making any form of standardisation difficult. They had regular contacts with ship breakers for supplies of second-hand engine parts and made frequent visits to Pounds' yard at Portsmouth and elsewhere.

A small office and workshop was established at Sheerness to deal with the inevitable paperwork and small repair jobs for the ships. Jack Whiting, his son Keith and stepsons Sid and David all took an active part in sailing and repairing the ships, although Jack came ashore more or less permanently shortly after taking over the *Pattree*. Jan originally worked out the wages and was also involved in storing the ships. She was particularly interested in cleanliness, carrying out thorough inspections of the accommodation as ships were acquired and ensuring that they were brought up to standard. Trevor Jewsbury, while still remaining a Trinity House pilot, looked after insurance, financial and administrative matters and occasionally did some relieving work afloat.

David had accompanied his step-father and served as mate of the *Borelly* but was eager for promotion. Jack, thinking that he was still too young and inexperienced, temporised and said that he would think about it when he had obtained his certificate. This David duly accomplished and rejoined the ship with his brand new certificate but Jack was still undecided. They loaded in the Old Harbour at Hull for Guernsey and Jack considered the matter on the way down the North Sea. The ship was passing the North East Spit off Margate about four in the morning and Jack asked the pilot boat if they could land one man from the ship. Getting an affirmative answer he called David and told him that he was promoted and promptly disembarked giving the sleepy young man the chance he had wanted.

## *Pattree* and *St. Andrews*

Two more ships were acquired at intervals of approximately two years, a plan that was aimed at gradually expanding the fleet without over-stretching the financial resources. By the time the second ship was acquired, payments on the first would be well in hand, and so on. There was generally little enough left at the end of the month when all the bills were paid, but the partners looked forward to taking their profit when the ships were eventually sold.

The two ships, *Pattree* (438/1957) and *St. Andrews* (437/1961), were acquired in 1977 and 1979 on five-year leases and were both products of the Hamburg shipbuilder J.J. Sietas. The *St. Andrews* had been owned earlier by Usborne and Son Ltd., a subsidiary of Buries Markes Ltd. who named their coasters after famous golf courses. For some reason the *Pattree* was a stiff ship and had a tendency to roll violently. They both had the usual problems associated with coastal shipping. The *St. Andrews* once had to be towed into the Tyne with her engine immobilised by a fishing net caught around the propeller. On one occasion when passing Fellows yard at Great Yarmouth, the *Pattree* was hit amidships by a yacht owned by a well-known turkey producer as it came out of the dry dock. The yacht's blame was clear and the owner asked to be sent the bill with somewhat less enthusiasm than he showed in his television advertisements. But nevertheless they were good, reliable ships and generally enjoyed good earnings.

When sold in 1988, the *St. Andrews* passed briefly through the hands of Caribbean owners before being sold to interests in Dubai. She capsized and sank while loading at Colombo in late 1992. Some months later she was raised and taken in tow for Mormugoa but disappeared on passage. In contrast, the departure of the *Pattree* in 1984 was more exotic. She was purchased by an architect, Arne Hasselqvist, who urgently needed a small vessel to take some high quality and expensive building materials from Marseilles to the island of Mustique. Since then she seems to have settled down to general trading in the Caribbean area.

## Fleet size

In order to maintain a reasonable level of income while remaining small enough to be able to control and manage the business without taking on extra shore staff, it was felt that the optimum fleet size would be six vessels. This effectively meant that at any one time they could expect to have five active ships available for work and one ship out for surveys or repairs. The ratio of 5 to 1 indicates a rather low utilisation factor and implies that the partners envisaged carrying out their repairs at the lowest possible cost. Ships were often placed on the public slipway at Ramsgate where costs were low and work could be effectively organised and controlled. This required their own close supervision and using local engineering concerns and subcontractors rather than using the larger shipyards where, although the time might be less, the costs would certainly be higher. It is all a question of priorities. However, as things transpired, in the period from 1985 to 1989 the company had nine ships and although the utilisation factor was higher, it was difficult to give the same

*Above: Pattree* on the River Trent *[C.A. Hill]. Below: St.Andrews* leaving Great Yarmouth in August 1973 whilst in Usborne ownership.

individual attention to each of the ships.

All the ships were under 500 gross tons and were thus not involved with the SOLAS Regulations and annual surveys. Even when keeping a ship fully equipped with properly maintained safety equipment, there are still considerable savings to be made by not having to stop the ship and pay for government surveys. All the ships' main engines were derated to below 750 kilowatts which enabled them to sail without an engineer. Apart from the *Malone*, which remained under the Irish flag, all the ships were under the British flag. The use of free flags was not nearly as popular or widespread as it later became but that is not to say that the company would have necessarily flagged out their ships. Indeed, it was frequently discussed but the terms of the leases forbade it.

*Woolacombe* in colours of R.W. Hurlock. *[C.A. Hill]*

Originally, masters, officers and ratings were all British and the company participated fully in the national training schemes. In later years, however, due to increased costs and a shortage of suitable British ratings, the company employed sailors from the Philippines, Cape Verde and elsewhere and formal training came to an end. In the early days the officers were paid according to the share system and received an agreed percentage of the ship's earnings less certain disbursements. This occasionally led to arguments and misunderstandings when the officers heard the gross freight figures and, without knowing the scale of the operating costs, imagined that considerable profits were being made at their expense. One of the masters was brought ashore to work in the office and was able to see the situation at first hand. He soon asked to return to sea and must have passed the word around because there were no more complaints. About 1980 the share system was phased out and replaced by a basic wage to which was added a cargo bonus. These cargo bonuses were paid on a sliding scale, increasing for each cargo carried during a calendar month. A 'long haul' allowance was paid to compensate for the extra time taken on voyages from, for example, Germany to Ireland.

### Woolacombe

After a gap of a year another vessel, *Woolacombe* (496/1967), was acquired in 1980. Being a few years younger than earlier units of the fleet, she was more lightly built in the modern style although fully up to classification society standards and still a fairly rugged workhorse. With her acquisition the company entered into leasing arrangements with Custodian Leasing Ltd. This

company had started in commercial window cleaning, extended into office cleaning and later into security work; hence the name when they entered the leasing business. The name was changed to Clientcare Finance Ltd. and subsequently Clientcare Ltd. when the security side was shed some years later.

Like most coastal vessels, the *Woolacombe* had her share of bumps and other damages. She had just had some bow damage repaired when, while berthing about a week later, she stemmed another quay. The master was adamant that the engine kept going ahead and would not go astern for him. The experts from Brons, the engine builders, checked everything and could find nothing wrong. In all probability the cause was much simpler and most masters have experienced it. When standing on the unaccustomed side of the engine controller, probably steering with the wandering lead unit, a mirror image situation is created and, in the heat of the moment, it is easy to apply the wrong movement to the engine. Rapid movements of the control lever are counter productive because there is always a short delay before the engine obeys the last command: if another command comes within the delay period the previous one is not obeyed and the cycle starts again.

At the end of the lease period Whitbury maintained nominal payments to Clientcare until 1990 when the ship was sold to a middle eastern buyer through his agent in Ipswich. Shortly afterwards, after loading a cargo of stone chippings at Dean Quarry for Whitstable, she was towed into Torquay with engine trouble and subsequently arrested. Apart from a few months in 1991 trading for a British company the ship laid at Torquay, alternately under arrest or repair until purchased by Sheik

Mohamed Farouk and Son Shipping in March 1994. Renamed *Lady Fazeela*, she finally sailed for Demerara, loaded with trucks, in July 1994 and is still trading in the Caribbean.

### Malone

The acquisition of the *Malone* (498/1962) occurred in a somewhat bizarre fashion. Concord Leasing acquired the ship from Shamrock Shipping Ltd. for leasing to a British company. Unbeknown to the leasing company, the manager later registered the vessel under the Honduran flag with the owner as Naviera Jade S. de R.L. and renamed her *Damita Joanne*. The lease payments were not maintained when the company went into liquidation and Concord finally traced the ship to Genoa. They re-possessed the ship and engaged a run crew to bring her back to Britain, changing the name at sea. She then laid at Boston pending a decision. Eventually, Concord and Whitbury came to an arrangement and in 1988 the latter took over the ship on advantageous terms thus breaking the established acquisition cycle.

As the ship was very dirty and not in the best condition it was decided to bring her to Rochester for cleaning and repairs. The trip south became exciting when a pipe in the engine room ruptured and nearly all the main engine lubricating oil was lost. However, once she had been cleaned up and the various problems rectified she performed very well in service.

It was discovered that the Honduran registry was only provisional and that the Irish registry had not been cancelled. This made it relatively simple to revert to the original name and port of registry, although the Irish authorities required a full survey. When owned by Shamrock Shipping the ship stood out by her master's insistence on painting her red instead of the standard Shamrock green. This upset the directors but they allowed him to continue and presumably still supplied him with the paint of his choice!

During 1989 *Malone* was shortened by just over a metre to bring her overall length below the 60 metre mark above which pilotage becomes compulsory. Without doubt, this action brought some good-natured criticism from Trevor Jewsbury's pilot colleagues. When the decision was made to sell the ship, it was thought an advantage to arrange another provisional registration under the Honduran flag. In the event, the new owner registered the ship in Cyprus and little benefit accrued.

### Reins

The *Reins* (496/1966) came from the same stable as the *Woolacombe*, built by Scheepswerf 'Voorwaarts' at Martenshoek, and managed by Wijnne & Barends of Delfzijl. She had been sold to Hurlocks of Ipswich before being acquired for the company in 1982. She remained with the company until 1989 when she was sold to James O'Neill who employed the same freight managers, Halcyon Shipping, as Whitbury. He moved the ship to his St. Vincent flag company, Tara Shipping Ltd., a year later. Sold in 1992 to Colombian owners she was renamed with the more hispanic-sounding *Rena* in a most economical style that would surely have met with approval from Whitbury. After a few years' trading in South America she sank with a cargo of sand and gravel.

*Reins [World Ship Society]*

### *Borelly* (2) and *Delce*

Both these ships were casualties of the Associated British Food Group's decision to divest itself of its fleet sailing under the banner of Weston Shipping. The two ships, *Jana Weston* (507/1971) and *Catrina Weston* (429/1971), were acquired by Custodian Leasing in 1984. Part of the sale agreement was that the ships should be renamed. This is quite a usual clause, particularly when the name has an obvious connection with the selling company or is part of a sequence of recognisable names in the sellers' house style. They were the only ships that Whitbury renamed. The appeal of their first ship's name *Borelly* is obvious but *Delce* is perhaps a little obscure to citizens living outside the Medway towns. In fact, it is the name of a road and an area of Rochester, the original home of the Whiting family, and lies to the west of Star Hill.

When purchased, the *Borelly* had a gross tonnage of 507. This did not suit Whitbury and, as they dispensed with the services of an engineer, they were able to take advantage of the rules and reallocate some of the space within the ship to reduce the gross tonnage to 499.99.

Neither ship was particularly successful and both were beset by a succession of minor engine problems, all largely cured by the time they were sold. *Borelly* was badly damaged while lying alongside and discharging at Howdendyke. The new tanker, *Eliza PG* (3,338/1992), coming down the Ouse from Selby, possibly a little late on the tide, was unable to negotiate the bend in the river and hit the ship on her starboard quarter.

The *Delce* was the first to go when she was sold to Captain Derick Goubert in 1990. He renamed her *Port Soif*, a geographical feature near his Guernsey home. She had an unfortunate incident in December 1993 when she struck a rock off Herm and sustained considerable bottom damage. After slipping at St. Sampson to ascertain the extent of the damage she was declared a constructive total loss. She was later sold to Simon Lyon-Smith of Teignmouth and towed to Plymouth. After a few months laid up there she was towed to Ramsgate where she was repaired on the slipway, renamed *Bahamas Provider* and sailed for the Caribbean in October 1994.

The *Borelly* lasted two years longer with the company and in 1992 was sold to the Parkside Warehousing and Transport Co. under the management of Genchem Marine Ltd. of Ipswich. During 1994 she arrived at Hull for surveys and repairs. These turned out to be considerably more expensive than anticipated and work was curtailed and the ship put into lay-up for some months with the repairs incomplete. Eventually she returned to service in late 1995.

### Sister ships from General Freight

Having prospered during the miners' strike of the mid-1980s by joining the fleet of British and foreign ships bringing coal from the continent to the British east coast ports, the company felt able to acquire yet more ships. With the Unilever plc decision to concentrate on core activities and sell off all their transport interests, several ships came on the market including those under the control of the General Freight Co. Ltd. Having decided to buy, it was important to Whitbury that the transactions took place before the end of March 1985 to keep within the financial year in order to take advantage of the prevailing capital allowances.

Two of the General Freight ships, the *Ellen W* (428/1974) and the *Freda W* (428/1974), were acquired by Custodian Leasing. They had an interesting history being originally completed for Mardorf Peach and Co. Ltd who became the managers when the ships were demise chartered to B.O.C.M. Silcocks Ltd. Under the management of Mardorf Peach the vessels operated on federated crew agreements, so that manning levels, wages and conditions became increasingly onerous. The decision was made to defederate the vessels and in an attempt to distance them from the past they were sold to another Unilever company and their names were changed. They were placed under the management of R. Lapthorn and Co. Ltd. who already operated a number of non-federated vessels. Both ships had always been well looked after and the majority of their cargoes had been grain, a commodity more kindly to a ship than many others.

The *Reins*, *Delce* and *Ellen W* were leased, not to Whitbury Shipping Co. Ltd., but to the associated Elmcrest Shipping Ltd. The major shareholders in Whitbury also held the majority of the shares in Elmcrest; control and management of the ships remained with Whitbury Shipping Co. Ltd.

The *Freda W* was sold in 1992 to the Great Western Shipping Co. Ltd. of Montserrat whose owner was a senior local politician, if not a former Prime Minister of the island. The *Ellen W* had the honour of being the last ship in Whitbury ownership when she was sold in 1993 to James O'Neill for his Tara Shipping Ltd. with Halcyon Shipping continuing to carry out the freight management.

### The final purchase

The last ship to be acquired by the company was the *River Tamar* (498/1981), also formerly owned by the General Freight Co. Ltd. She had been built at Wivenhoe and her managers had always been F.T. Everard and Sons Ltd. Early in her career with Whitbury she had a near calamity when, loaded with rice for Rainham, she struck some barges in Mucking Reach. Although the ship's side plating was damaged, the inner bulkhead of the wing ballast tank was not penetrated and the ingress of water was limited to the forecastle and the cargo remained dry.

*River Tamar* had other problems, not of her own making, the fault being that she just happened to be at the wrong place at the wrong time. Once, lying on the Park Quay in Rotterdam, another ship struck her causing sufficient damage for it to be necessary to go to the Van Brink shipyard for repairs. A similar incident occurred at Selby and yet another at New Holland when a Swedish ship parted a backspring while manoeuvring to leave the berth and ran into her. The repairs were all covered by the insurance but such incidents are upsetting, cause delays and add to the already considerable stress of ship operation.

Perhaps the most newsworthy but saddest incident occurred when she was sailing from

identified the possibility of world wide trade with small ships, notably as carried out by the Danes. The ships would have to be somewhat larger than their existing fleet, probably 'tween deckers, and be more comprehensively equipped. They would certainly cost more to lease, operate and maintain. The crew, with foreign-going qualifications, would expect higher wages than their coastal counterparts. Finance was becoming more of a problem, particularly when the Government withdrew the first-year investment allowances. It soon became apparent that the scale of the investment, for either plan, would be beyond anything they had managed previously and the term of any loans or leases would put completion well into the future. New ships were out of the question and quite soon they realised that good quality second-hand ships would require an investment beyond their means and loans would commit them to more years than they cared to consider.

Zeebrugge on 6th March 1987. She was amongst the first ships on the scene of the *Herald Of Free Enterprise* tragedy. Her master, who later received an official commendation, held his ship's bow onto the stricken ferry while his crew jumped aboard. They managed to rescue twelve people, including a baby, before returning to Zeebrugge to pick up medical staff and supplies for the full rescue operation.

Although commercially disappointing, *River Tamar* was a good little ship but when loaded she presented a very low profile and great care had to be taken to prevent sea water entering the bunker tanks via the air pipes. She was the first of the company's former General Freight ships to be sold when she went to Ramsey Steamship Co. Ltd. in late 1990.

**Whither Whitbury?**

After the frenetic days during the miner's strike and the later ship purchases, the partners settled down to consider the future. They had formed the opinion that the truly profitable days for small British coastal vessels were numbered and that, if they were to remain in business, a change of direction would be necessary. Both of them were very close to the sea and ideally placed to notice the trends and the apparently profitable employment of other shipowners.

They thought of larger coastal ships and also

With this realisation, coupled with the fact that neither really wanted to establish a shipping empire, the owners came to the conclusion that it was probably best to call it a day. Thus, in 1987 they decided not to acquire any more ships and to sell off their fleet as suitable offers were made. In the event, the last ship was sold in 1993 just nineteen years after the first one was acquired in 1974. During this time they had owned eleven ships altogether with a peak of nine ships in 1985-88, managed the ships safely, efficiently and economically with no major disasters in truly hands-on style, and dealt with all their crew, repairs and maintenance matters directly without any outside assistance. Throughout they ignored the siren voices of the free flags and remained true to the British flag with the lone Irish exception. Until 1987 when they decided to sell the ships they had shouldered their responsibility towards the training of young British seafarers. It was all quite a feat and, although perhaps not unique, the company is a fine example of what can be achieved with experience, hard work and the will to succeed.

*The fleet list of Whitbury Shipping Co. Ltd. with further photographs will appear in the next edition*

# TWO-FUNNEL TANKERS
## David Burrell

Although the existence of petroleum has been known for millenia, the modern oil age is generally considered to have started in August 1859 when the self-styled Colonel Edwin Drake drilled a well at Titusville, Pennsylvania.

Production was initially small and transport was effected in barrels. The first full cargo of oil to Britain was by the 224-ton brig *Elizabeth Watts* commanded by Captain C. Bryant, which arrived in the Thames on 7th January 1862. The Customs Bill of Entry recorded her cargo as 301 barrels rock oil consigned to 'order', 100 barrels coal oil for Coats and Co. and 328 barrels coal oil to Herzog and Co.

Shipping in casks was both expensive and dangerous. Not only did leakage lose cargo but the resultant fumes were highly dangerous and led to the loss of some ships by explosion and fire. Several went missing and the cause of their loss was not established, although their cargo was highly suspect. In the years that followed many ideas were developed for the bulk carriage of liquid oil, some ships being converted by the fitting of tanks in their holds and others being built new with integral tanks.

What is considered to be the first modern tanker, from which all later ships could trace ancestry, took to the water in 1885. Named *Gluckauf* and delivered to German owners, she was quickly followed by a sister *Vorwarts*. The following year came *Bakuin* for British owners. For many years the world tanker fleet remained small when compared to cargo vessels. In 1900 *Lloyd's Register* lists 174 steam and 19 sailing tankers totalling 424,938gt. The years between the World Wars saw rapid growth in oil consumption, but it was to be the second half of the twentieth century before oil finally ousted coal and the tanker fleet assumed its major role in shipping.

In this period only six two-funnel tankers with fore and aft stacks have been identified, that is unless you know better. In saying this I apply the same criteria as was adopted in *Record* 7 when the two-funnel cargo liners article commenced. The most obvious group of ships this excludes are the whale factory ships which adopted abreast funnels to permit a stern ramp. Some even had four funnels and were covered in the series on whaling ships commenced in *Record* 5.

First of the two-funnel tankers was launched on the Tyne by Palmers for the American Petroleum Co.,Rotterdam. Like many of the early tankers that avoided serious casualties the *Rotterdam* had a long life, passing to Italian owners in 1926 who renamed her *Olandese*, as which she went to the breakers in 1932.

*Rotterdam*, with a flag at each mast. *[George Scott collection]*

*Rotterdam*, by now with only one funnel, is seen as *Olandese* when owned in Genoa between 1926 and 1932 (top). *[National Maritime Museum P14503]*

*Buyo Maru* (middle) in later life became Shell's *Delphinula*, seen here in the Hamoaze at Plymouth on 7th April 1933 (bottom). She spent the last ten years of her life as a storage hulk. *[Middle: Peter Newall collection; bottom: National Maritime Museum N10698]*

Three two-funnel tankers entered service in 1908-1909 and give the impression of coincidence as they appear to be individual orders. But research brings all three together into a series of orders placed by H.E. Moss and Co., Liverpool - two from Armstrong, Whitworth and Co. Ltd., and one from Swan, Hunter and Wigham Richardson Ltd.

The first, when nearing completion, was sold through the agency of Lawther, Latta and Co. to Toyo Kisen Kabushiki Kaisha, Yokohama, and entered service as *Buyo Maru*, one of the first Japanese flag tankers. She returned to the British flag in 1915 when bought by the Anglo-Saxon Petroleum Co. Ltd. acting on behalf of the Admiralty. Tankers were at a premium during the war and she was renamed *Delphinula* and identified as Fleet Oiler 188. As such she was torpedoed and damaged by *U 63* in August 1918, being beached in Suda Bay. After the war she continued to serve the Royal Navy until hulked at Alexandria in 1936. Two years later she moved to Gibraltar in a similar role which continued until her sale to Spanish breakers late in 1946. In September 1947 she arrived at Pasajes and was demolished.

*Cheyenne* on trials. *[Ian Rae collection]*

The second ship delivered, Swan Hunter's order, was also sold and entered service as *Cheyenne* in the British fleet of the Anglo-American Oil Co. Ltd. Surviving the war she stranded at St Monans, Fife, on 11th November 1924. Outward bound from Grangemouth in ballast for the United States, she was refloated but the extent of damage dictated her sale for breaking up, which took place at Bo'ness.

The third of the Moss orders was the only one to hoist their flag when delivered in February 1909 as *Lucigen*, owned by the Lucigen Steam Ship Co. Ltd. She gave over thirty years of service before joining *Delphinula* in Admiralty service. They purchased her in 1940 and she took up station at Lagos as a fuelling hulk. With the return of peace in 1945 she became redundant, so in June or July 1946 was towed out by the Nigerian Marine tug *Lagos Atlas* (507/1918) and sunk by scuttling charges on the 100-fathom line, about 25 miles offshore.

*Lucigen* at Preston (opposite bottom and this page top).

*Santa Rita* (middle: note the 'U' between the funnels) and *Santa Maria* (bottom). *[Both: Peter Newall collection]*

The other two funnel tankers were sisters completed in 1902 at the Cleveland yard of the American Shipbuilding Co. as *Minnetonka* and *Minnewaska*. With a length of 430 feet they were dry cargo ships intended for service on the Geat Lakes. In 1906 they were sold to Californian interests and left the Lakes, which would have entailed cutting them in two as the Welland and Lachine Canals, through which they would have to pass to reach the sea, could only take vessels up to 255 feet. They were renamed *Santa Barbara* and *Santa Rita* and converted into oil tankers to work for Union Oil Co.

Their service was not limited to the North Pacific. *Santa Maria* was on passage with fuel from Philadelphia to Glasgow when torpedoed by the German submarine *U 19* on 25th February 1918 off the north east coast of Ireland in position 55.14 north, 6.9 west. *Santa Rita* survived her sister for a few years. She was last seen on 23rd October 1921 off Key West on a voyage with oil from New Orleans to Spezia. She was posted missing at Lloyd's on 18th January 1922.

# PORT LINE'S GOLDEN ERA
## Peter Newall

Between 1949 and 1961 Port Line took delivery of fourteen new ships which must rate among the finest refrigerated cargo ships to operate under the British flag. These handsome ships were always immaculate and their introduction reinforced Port Line's reputation as one of the most prestigious shipping lines on the Australian and New Zealand service in the 1950s and 1960s.

**PORT AUCKLAND** (top)
*Hawthorn, Leslie and Co. Ltd., Newcastle-on-Tyne; 1949, 11,945gt, 560 feet overall*
*Two Doxford-type oil engines 6-cyl. 2SCSA by Hawthorn, Leslie and Co. Ltd., Newcastle-on-Tyne*
When *Port Auckland* and her Swan, Hunter-built sister *Port Brisbane* were completed in 1949 they generated a huge amount of interest because of their modern design and complete contrast to the rather dowdy looking British cargo liners of the day. With their long forecastle, streamlined bridge front and funnel, they created a unique image for Port Line on the Australian and New Zealand run and looked like small passenger liners even though they only carried 12 passengers. Cargo was carried in six holds, five of which were insulated, and they were among the first British ships to be fitted with a crane which was situated aft between Nos 4 and 5 hatches. In 1976, still partly owned by Port Line, *Port Auckland* was converted into the sheep carrier *Mashaalah* for service between Australia and the Middle East and in 1979 was scrapped at Kaohsiung, Taiwan. [*Peter Newall Collection*]

**PORT TOWNSVILLE** (middle)
*Swan, Hunter and Wigham Richardson Ltd, Newcastle-on-Tyne; 1951, 8,681gt, 489 feet overall*
*Doxford-type oil engine 6-cyl. 2SCSA by Wallsend Slipway and Engineering Co., Newcastle-on-Tyne*
In 1951 three single-screw vessels were completed for the company, *Ports Adelaide, Townsville,* and *Nelson.* Although the basic layout was similar, each came from a different yard and had a differing appearance. *Port Townsville* looked like a smaller version of the 1949 pair but with a shorter forecastle

and an extended bridge deck which became a feature of most of the following ships. All three were sold for scrap in 1972 following the take-over of the Cunard Group by Trafalgar House. [*M. R. Dippy*]

**PORT NELSON** (bottom)
*Harland and Wolff Ltd., Belfast; 1951, 8,950gt, 490 feet overall*
*Oil engine 7-cyl. 2SCSA by Harland and Wolff Ltd., Belfast*
The first in the series to be built by Harland and Wolff, *Port Nelson* (seen here during a Clan Line charter) was similar to *Port Townsville* but with a more conventional modern design. [*Alex Duncan*]

**PORT SYDNEY** (top)
*Swan, Hunter and Wigham Richardson Ltd, Newcastle-on-Tyne; 1955, 10,166gt, 533 feet overall*
*Two oil engines 6-cyl. 2SCSA by Wallsend Slipway and Engineering Co. Ltd., Newcastle-on-Tyne*
*Port Melbourne* and *Port Sydney* were slightly smaller versions of *Port Auckland* and *Port Brisbane* but with less streamlining. Their design also included a shorter forecastle, extended bridge deck, and a tripod signal mast above the bridge. They were also the first Port Line ships to have anchors which fitted into a recess and, like most of the modern post-war design vessels, they also had one heavy lift derrick and a crane. In 1972 both were sold to the Greek shipowner John Carras and converted beyond recognition into cruise ships. *Port Sydney* became *Daphne* and was renamed *Switzerland* in 1997. [Peter Newall Collection]

**PORT MELBOURNE** (middle) and **DANAE** (bottom)
*Harland and Wolff Ltd., Belfast; 1955, 10,470gt, 533 feet overall*
*Two oil engines 6-cyl. 2SCSA by Harland and Wolff Ltd., Belfast*
The Belfast-built sister of *Port Sydney* differed mainly in the design of the signal mast and the shaping of the hances at the forward end of the promenade deck. In 1969 *Port Melbourne* operated the inaugural service for Compass Line - a joint Blue Star-Port Line service between Australia and South Africa: note their funnel markings. *Port Melbourne* was rebuilt as the 412-capacity cruiseship *Danae* - seen in the bottom photograph leaving Cape Town - and today continues to sail as *Princess Danae*. [Middle: Peter Newall Collection; bottom: Ian Shiffman]

**PORT MONTREAL** as **PUERTO PRINCESA** (top)
*Harland and Wolff Ltd., Govan; 1954, 7,179gt, 469 feet overall*
*Oil engine 7-cyl. 2SCSA by Harland and Wolff Ltd., Govan*
*Port Montreal* was a one-off designed, as her name implies, for the MANZ Line (Montreal, Australia and New Zealand Line Ltd., a joint service formed in 1936 and operated by Port Line, New Zealand Shipping and Ellerman and Bucknall) and the smallest of the 14 ships built for the company between 1949 and 1961). In 1957 Crusader Shipping Co. Ltd. was formed by the four conference lines to operate services to alternative markets for New Zealand goods, which were then heavily dependent on the United Kingdom. *Port Montreal* was transferred to the Crusader New Zealand-Japan service. In the Trafalgar House 'cull' of 1972 she was sold to a Phillipine-based company and renamed *Puerto Princesa*, as seen here. Six years later, after a collision at Manila, she was condemned and sold to Taiwanese breakers. [Peter Newall Collection]

**PORT LAUNCESTON** (middle)
*Harland and Wolff Ltd., Govan; 1957, 8,957gt, 491 feet overall*
*Oil engine 7-cyl. 2SCSA by Harland and Wolff Ltd., Govan*
Enlarged versions of *Port Nelson*, both *Port Launceston* and *Port Invercargill* had a signal mast above the bridge, a truncated mast with heavy derrick on the forecastle in place of a pair of kingposts and derricks instead of cranes at No 3 hatch. In 1977 *Port Launceston* was sold to Woburn Shipping of Singapore and renamed *United Vantage*. In 1980, she too ended up at Taiwanese scrapyard. [Peter Newall Collection]

**PORT INVERCARGILL** (bottom)
*Harland and Wolff Ltd., Govan; 1957, 8,847gt, 491 feet overall*
*Oil engine 7-cyl. 2SCSA by Harland and Wolff Ltd., Govan*
Unlike her sister, *Port Invercargill's* career with Port Line was short. In June 1967, along with a number of other ships, she was trapped in Great Bitter Lake whilst transiting the Suez Canal at the time of the Egypt-Israel War. Declared a constructive total loss, she was released in 1975 and sold to Greek owners who renamed her *Kavo Kolones* - four years later she was broken up in Taiwan. [Peter Newall Collection]

**PORT NEW PLYMOUTH** (top)

*Swan, Hunter and Wigham Richardson Ltd, Newcastle-on-Tyne; 1960, 13,085gt, 561 feet overall*

*Two Sulzer-type oil engines 6-cyl. 2SCSA by Wallsend Slipway and Engineering Co. Ltd., Newcastle-on-Tyne*

Between 1960 and 1962 Port Line took delivery of the two largest ships built for the company. The first of these, *Port New Plymouth*, came from Swan, Hunter, the yard which had designed the trend-setting and attractive *Port Brisbane* eleven years earlier. Ironically, the 1960 vessel turned out to be the most unattractive of all the post-war Port Line ships with its disproportionately small funnel. She was also the first of the larger ships not to have cranes and had a raised poop deck, which included No. 6 hatch. In 1967 *Port New Plymouth* carried a single container to Melbourne as an experiment - this new form of cargo management, of course, spelt the end of traditional ships like *Port New Plymouth* and in 1979 she was sold to Kaohsiung breakers. *[Peter Newall Collection]*

**PORT NICHOLSON** (bottom)

*Harland and Wolff Ltd., Belfast; 1962, 13,847gt, 573 feet overall*

*Two Burmeister & Wain-type oil engines 6-cyl. 2SCSA by Harland and Wolff Ltd., Govan*

In 1962, the biggest of all Port Line ships to date, *Port Nicholson*, was certainly better looking than *Port New Plymouth* and at the time also had the world's largest refrigerated cargo capacity (almost 600,000 cubic feet). She too had a premature end when she went for scrap in 1979. *[Peter Newall Collection]*

**PORT ST LAWRENCE** (middle)

*Harland and Wolff Ltd., Belfast; 1961, 9,040 gt, 500 feet overall*

*Oil engine 7-cyl. 2SCSA by Harland and Wolff Ltd., Belfast*

The last two conventional Port Line designed cargo ships, *Port St Lawrence* and *Port Alfred* were intended for the MANZ Line service. With a service speed of 17 knots, they carried 10 passengers and were broadly similar to *Port Launceston* and *Port Invercargill* except for the pair of kingposts forward of No. 3 hatch. In 1975, the two sisters were transferred to Cunard-Brocklebank, *Port St Lawrence* being renamed *Matangi*. Three years later, Port Line ceased to exist as a separate entity within the Cunard Group. Sold out of the fleet in 1982, she was scrapped the following year at Gadani Beach as *Nordave*. *[Peter Newall Collection]*

# TORQUAY HARBOUR IN THE THIRTIES: Part 1
## David Eeles

Torquay harbour in the post-war years would not have struck most holidaymakers or even residents as being exactly a hive of commercial shipping activity. There was an all-too-brief flurry of activity in the 1970s and early 1980s as Graham Thompsons' Torbay Seaways strove to re-establish ferry and freight links with the Channel Islands using a variety of interesting vessels. The occasional medium-sized coaster has graced Haldon Pier, in with pumice for a local firm of blockmakers, rock salt for the roads, and ammonium nitrate as fertilizer. Apart from this, Torquay harbour has been synonymous with pleasure craft, as perhaps befits its premier holiday resort status.

**Early days**

However, it was not always thus. The construction of what is now the inner harbour in the early years of the nineteenth century was prompted by purely commercial considerations to provide not only landing facilities for the growing numbers of visitors to what was becoming a fashionable resort, but also to import the ever-increasing quantity of bulky building materials, coal and many other sundry goods required by a community that was expanding at the rate of 5,000 a decade between the years 1841 and 1871. The burgeoning town was served by a steam packet service to London as early as the 1820s, and by the mid-nineteenth century Torquay, like many other West Country ports, was able to boast trans-Atlantic links. The local timber merchant and shipowner Thomas Crossman used his little vessels of around 250 tons to bring timber from Canada and on the return trip take emigrants, for the princely sum of around £3. The front dustjacket of Michael Bouquet's seminal book on Britain's vanished small harbours, *No Gallant Ship*, is adorned with a photograph of Crossman's attractive miniature full-rigger, probably the *Margaret* (261 tons, built in Nova Scotia in 1826), sitting high and dry at Torquay with all sail set. The first two photographs depict what is now Torquay's inner harbour in the nineteenth century.

In terms of numbers of vessels, the late nineteenth century and Edwardian period was probably the heyday of trade through Torquay harbour, despite the coming of the railway in 1848 which resulted in the loss of most

Although *Emily* is a common name, this is almost certainly the 152-ton, 84-feet long, two-masted brigantine of the name built at Prince Edward Island in 1848. At the time of the photograph she was owned by Henry Manley and Co., listed in the 1878/9 *White's Directory* as being a shipowner and coal merchant of Victoria Parade, the quay she is lying alongside. In the 1881 census Henry Manley is listed as being born in Exeter 60 years previously, married, with five sons and one daughter. One wonders if Henry or his sons are the ones shown tarring the hull in the photograph. *[Torquay Museum]*

This view of North Quay looking towards Vaughan Parade appears to show the *Emily* again, presumably unloading coal which was at that time stored in the adjacent sheds. Ahead of her are two similar vessels that seem to have almost completed discharge. In the earlier days of sail some of these colliers were able to load a back freight of limestone from the many quarries in and around Torquay for the iron-smelting furnaces of the north east. The uncompleted tower of St. Johns Church on the right of the picture allows us to date it to between 1871 and 1883. Most of the area to the left of the still-extant banjo at the end of the quay was filled in to become part of Princess Gardens in 1893. The building displaying the unusual sobriquet 'British Workman No. 1' was a teetotal working man's hostel. *[Torquay Museum]*

passenger traffic and the withdrawal of the packet service linking Torquay with Bristol Channel ports. Regular coastal liner services, including a London to Bristol/Cardiff service via Torquay, Plymouth and sometimes Teignmouth, continued, however, even into the 1930s, under the umbrella of Coast Lines.

**Indian summer**

Due to the efforts of two men, one an anonymous photographer and the other an undergraduate of Exeter University, Wilfred Hore, it is now possible to piece together evidence which indicates that Torquay may well have enjoyed an Indian summer in the late 1920s and early 1930s during which tonnages through the port may even have exceeded figures from earlier periods. Although comparisons between the nineteenth century and inter-war years are difficult, it is interesting to note that total imports into the Teignmouth customs area, which included Torquay and Brixham, were 67,800 tons in 1865 and 108,000 tons in 1905. This compares with 65,102 tons landed in Torquay alone in 1927, the peak year of the period 1924-1935.

Thanks to Wilfred Hore's detailed account of the trade of Torquay Harbour 1924-1935, using statistics supplied by the Harbour Master, but which regrettably do not appear to have survived in their original form, it is possible to build up quite a comprehensive picture of trade in this picturesque, if somewhat incongruous, setting. The photographs, apparently taken mostly in the mid to late 1930s but unfortunately rarely dated, supply further insight into the vessels involved in this trade. They show an amazing variety of ships, as befits what was a transitory period in coastal shipping, before sail and steam finally gave way completely to motorships. Nineteenth century steam colliers could still be seen alongside modern motor coasters, and auxiliary sailing ships still fought a rearguard battle in certain trades against the ubiquitous Dutch motor coasters and larger timber ships.

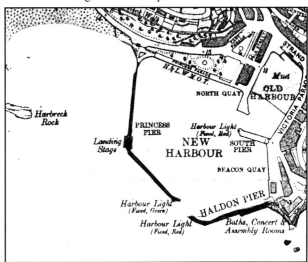

Torquay Inner Harbour

The smart coastal liners of the Coast Lines fleet were undoubtedly the aristocrats of the harbour scene as recorded by our unknown photographer in the 1930s, and none more so than the veteran *Moray Coast* (677/1905) (top). She was built by Caledon at Dundee in 1905 as the *Princess Helena* for Langlands, a Glasgow-based company taken over by Coast Lines in 1919 as part of their extensive Royal Mail-financed expansion. Renamed *Moray Coast* in 1920, she served the company until replaced by more modern tonnage in 1935, although she went on to work briefly under the Greek flag before reverting to the British flag. Her final service was to be sunk as a blockship at Dunkirk in 1940. As the photograph shows, Coast Lines had their own warehouse on Beacon Quay in the outer harbour that was demolished only in the 1960s.

The more classic coastal liner profile of the *Yorkshire Coast* (702/1913) is shown to good effect as she threads her way towards Beacon Quay through what would now be called the classic yachts of the period (middle). The entrance to the harbour is just out of the picture to the left, while behind Princess Pier can be seen houses spreading up the hillside from Paignton.

      The *Yorkshire Coast* was built for the London Welsh Steam Ship Co. Ltd. as the *Llanelly Trader* by the Dundee Shipbuilding Co., coming under the Coast Lines' unbrella in 1923. Becoming the *Solin* under the Yugoslav flag in 1938 she was seized by Italy in 1941 only to be recaptured by Yugoslavia in 1943. Despite these adventures she soldiered on and achieved her half-century before being broken up at Split in 1963.

The depression years of the 1930s helped render the older steamers uneconomic, and the *Hampshire Coast* (485/1937) is representative of the new generation of motor ships that replaced them (opposite bottom). She was one of six (out of a pre-war total of 20) motorships built in Holland at the De Noord yard at Alblasserdam. In 1946 she briefly became the *Springhaven* of Springwell Shipping Co. Ltd. and then in 1947 the *Gannochy* of Dundee, Perth and London Shipping Co. Ltd., until she foundered in the Mersey Channel in 1958 carrying stone from Penmaenmawr to Liverpool.

Pictured at Beacon Quay, but providing something of a contrast to the Coast Lines vessels, is the 373-gross *Charlus*, built 1917 (above). She does, rather surprisingly given the predominance of British shipyards at building steam coasters, have something in common with the *Hampshire Coast*, in that she was also built in a Dutch yard, in this case van der Kuy and van der Ree's yard in Rotterdam, as the *Princenhage II* for Dutch owners. At the time the photograph was taken she was owned by James M. Piggins of Montrose, raising the possibility that she may have been unloading seed potatoes from that part of Scotland. She survived the Second World War to be scrapped in 1953.

## General cargo

In the thirties regular coastal liner traffic had still to be completely supplanted by the railways. Hore attributes the survival of this trade partly to a Government subsidy for coastwise shipping, but apart from a brief period of subsidy towards the end of the First World War that was designed to counteract the port congestion that was ironically caused partly by unrealistic subsidies to the railways, the author has been unable to find any evidence of subsidies in the 1920s. Trim Coast Lines' vessels still called at Torquay, generally on Saturday evenings, en route for other south west ports and then Swansea, with calls made at Bristol and Newport by inducement. The return trip was generally from Swansea direct to London with tinplate or, in the spring, coffee from Avonmouth. The vessels generally took two weeks per round trip, and regular callers in the early 1930s included the steamships *Cambrian Coast* (773/1922), *Gloucester Coast* (919/1913), *Moray Coast* (677/1905) and *Yorkshire Coast* (702/1913). These vessels carried a wide variety of general goods, and Hore's figures show that, unlike most of the other goods traded through Torquay, the tonnage of general cargo (sometimes including small consignments of cement) continued to grow throughout the period, starting at under 500 tons in 1924 and peaking in 1935 at over 3,200 tons. This surprising growth, at a time when railways were becoming ever faster and more efficient but before the roads had improved to a level to allow long-distance road travel to compete effectively, was made up of an interesting miscellany of goods including groceries (mainly sugar and golden syrup), flour, groundnut oil, fancy timber, marble, glass, asphalt, and oilcake for cattle feed. The marble imports were for the local Jenkins Marble Works, which finally closed in 1996. They illustrate an interesting shortfall in the facilities offered at Torquay, since neither dockside cranes nor ships' derricks could cope with lifts greater than three tons. At that time, most of the larger blocks, imported from Italy via London, of necessity came by rail. The hinterland served by Torquay for these general commodities extended as far as Exeter and Seaton in the east and Totnes in the west, considerably farther than was the case with most of the other cargoes imported. As well as general commodities, the Coast Lines' vessels also imported large quantities of materials for the tannery and wool mill operated by Messrs. Vicary at Newton Abbot, five miles inland. Although undoubtedly founded on the local wool trade, Vicarys, first established in 1747, had long since come to depend on raw wool and dried sheepskins from Australia, South Africa and New Zealand, imported via London. The wool was sorted, washed, carded and combed in south Devon, then sent to Yorkshire by road for spinning and weaving. Tallow and quebracho, a tanning extract imported from South Africa via London, and the even more exotic ostrich skins (tanned and dressed before being sent to London or Walsall to be made into bags) made up the remainder of materials related to this trade, which accounted for 11,961 tons over the period of the survey, or 2.1% of the total. Teignmouth was also involved in this trade, and competition between the two ports may have helped account for quite large annual fluctuations.

## Building materials

The general cargo imported by Coast Lines may have accounted for the more valuable commodities, but by far the greater volume of imports were of cheap bulk goods where sea transport still had a considerable advantage over rail. The largest category of goods were those destined for the building industry. At this stage in its development, Torquay as a premier holiday destination was responding to the vast improvement to the rail links and the almost universal adoption of paid holiday periods for the industrial masses of the North. This, together with a Government measure guaranteeing building societies against loss, stimulated a building boom which sucked in copious quantities of sand, cement, timber, plaster, bricks, slates and tiles. Together these accounted for 65% of the total

tonnage landed, although it could be said that this figure is somewhat artificially inflated when it is realised that 29.3% (168,894 tons) of that total was sand, dredged only five miles (as the crow flies) away on the River Dart. This commodity illustrates how quickly road transport was to make huge incursions into seaborne trade. In this case the sand was dredged several miles up the River Dart near Galmpton and taken approximately ten miles around the coast to Torquay for use by the Council and other builders by three small wooden yawls with auxiliary paraffin oil motors, owned by F.T. Langmead and Sons. However, the tonnage loaded had decreased from a maximum of over 19,000 tons in 1926 to only 9,500 in 1935. With building sites outside Torquay already being supplied direct by lorry from Galmpton, Langmeads were experimenting with

extending this service to Torquay itself, and sure enough the yawls were eventually relegated to dredging work exclusively.

After sand and coal, cement in bulk came third in the total number of tons landed between 1924-35, and was one of the few commodities to show an increase over these years, from about 5,000 tons in 1924 to over 10,550 in 1935. This is accounted for by the relatively dense nature of the product, and the fact that most of it came from the London area, over 200 miles away. For this type of goods sea transport was to remain competitive for many more years, but through Teignmouth rather than Torquay in the post-war period. Some was shipped in on the regular Coast Lines' service, and it is believed that Coast Lines may have chartered in some of the small motor vessels (85-100 tons) and steam vessels (140-150 tons) which photographs record being unloaded by their warehouse on Beacon Quay. A small amount of cement was imported from Antwerp and Ghent in Dutch vessels, which also brought some plaster.

In the early 1930s sand for Torquay's builders was dredged and bought round from Galmpton in the River Dart by a small fleet of wooden auxiliary ketches owned by the Langmead family. The photograph opposite shows their 54-ton *Mizpah*, built by Date's at Kingsbridge for the Plymouth-based Roose family over 100 years ago in 1898, waiting for the next trip against the rather incongruous background of the smart shops on the Strand and the even smarter Regency facade of The Terrace above them. As detailed in the fascinating *Lost Ships of the Westcountry*, by Martin Langley and Edwina Small, her remains can still be seen but about 250 miles apart - her hull lies slowly disintegrating in Mill Creek near Dartmouth, while her pump windlass is in the National Maritime Museum.

The small steamer *Snowcrete* (351/1921) was owned between 1929 and 1936 by the Cement Marketing Co. Ltd., London, in whose colours she is seen on South Pier (right). This company sold the famous Blue Circle brand of cement. The *Snowcrete* was to cheat the breakers yard, sinking under the name *Warren Grove* on 9th November 1948 off Montrose as a result of her coal cargo shifting in heavy weather. Sadly, only three of her crew were rescued. A similar vessel and fleetmate of the Snowcrete, the *Hartford* (407/1912), is also recorded unloading cement in Torquay, a cargo which as Captain 'Harry' Bagshaw relates in his epic *Coasting Sailorman*, was often bought to the resort by Thames sailing barges in the previous decade. One wonders if the crew members manning the ratlines and standing on the foremast crosstrees of the *Snowcrete* were using skills learnt in that hard trade.

The *Lady Sophia* (232/1938) was one of several Faversham-built motor vessels belonging to the long-established Rochester firm of Thomas Watson, who, like most of the Thames and Medway based owners, were originally sailing barge operators (above). Watsons' barges regularly traded down-channel as far as Torquay and even Truro with cement, usually returning with china or ball clay. The light-blue hulled *Lady Sophia* appears to be continuing this trade, unloading cement on to builders' merchants

William Thomas' lorries on Beacon Quay. This company's latter-day coasters, looking rather more sober but still very smart with charcoal grey hulls and colourfully banded funnels, were still regularly to be seen loading clay in nearby Teignmouth until very recently.

*Lady Sophia* was sold in 1957 to Norwegian owners, first becoming *Sjøholm* and in 1963 *Nordia*. She was sunk off Szczecin after a collision on 11th October 1979.

Perhaps the most obtrusive building-related import into Torquay was timber. Stacks of sawn and planed planks could be seen along Beacon Quay and Haldon Pier, often with their consignees boards - the old-established but by now diversified builders' merchant Crossmans to the fore - proclaiming ownership. Around 5,000 tons a year on average was imported between 1924 and 1935 mostly from the Baltic states in Swedish, Danish and Norwegian vessels. Hore claims that British vessels were not employed in this trade partly because of a tariff against them and partly because of the expertise that the Scandinavians had developed in this specialist trade. Nevertheless, one photograph does show the 1938-built Hull-registered *Mytongate* unloading timber on Beacon Quay. Many of the vessels often unloaded only part of their cargoes at Torquay, the rest going to places such as Margate, Ramsgate and Cowes. However, Hore notes that Torquay was far from an ideal port for timber. There was a lack of storage space, and one photograph shows the 1917-built Swedish timber ship *Mercurius* having to wait for the annual Regatta fair, then held on Beacon Quay, to finish before unloading could commence. The other constraint was lack of water for the larger vessels increasingly being used - the maximum for Torquay was 300 standards, which compared with between 500-1,000 standards at Plymouth, which had a regular monthly service from Sweden. Avonmouth also had a regular service to Danzig, as well as being the terminal port for competing shipments of Canadian pine. Despite the increasing competition by road from both these ports as well as Totnes, Teignmouth and Exmouth, Torquay was still able to supply a hinterland from North Devon to Sidmouth and even Plymouth for at least some of their requirements.

The trade in bricks only featured during the building boom years between 1924 and 1930, and was a good example of Government reflationary measures causing temporary regional shortages until extra local capacity, eventually totaling six brickworks in or near Torquay, came on stream. Slate and tile imports also peaked in these boom years, although small quantities of around 500 tons a year continued to be handled in the early 1930s. Welsh slates brought from Bangor by small British coasting vessels competed with rail-borne Cornish slates which formed the bulk of supply to the district.

*To be continued.*

The timber ships were the largest auxiliary sailing vessels recorded in the harbour. Here the *Johannes* displaces the colliers from their usual berth on South Pier (right).

There are several auxiliary *Johannes* listed in *Lloyd's Register* for the inter-war years, and the help of readers is requested to decide which one is shown here. No flag is visible, and the identification must be based on knowledge of which countries' ship-building tradition she fits most closely.

Most of the timber, however, seems to have been bought by elderly Scandinavian steamers, of which the Norwegian *Sigrid* (965/1920) is a classic example, albeit she was built in Holland (below). Dutch builders made the most of their country's neutrality during and just after the First World War, and built not just sailing, steam and motor coasters, but also larger ships. Completed as *Nystrand*, she was acquired by Bachke and Co. of Trondheim in 1923 and renamed *Sigrid*, carrying this name right through the Second World War, when she was managed in Llanelly, until 1950. For the next eight years she was in German ownership, as *Dietrich Oldendorff* and as *Signal*, until broken up at Lubeck late in 1958.

On the hillside to the left behind Haldon Pier can be seen the impressive original facade of the Imperial Hotel, now completely concealed by post-war modernisation.

# POLSKAROB
## Jerzy Swieszkowski and Bohdan Huras

The beginning and ending of the story of POLSKAROB was closely entwined with the changing fortunes of the state of Poland itself and, before telling it, a little historical background may be appropriate.

Following the fall of the Elected Kingdom of Poland in the late 18th century, the country was partitioned by three surrounding empires: the Prussian, the Austro-Hungarian, and the Czarist Russian. One result was a lack of industrialisation, except in the German-held portion where the Silesian coalfield was developed around the town of Katowice.

Although the end of the First World War saw only modest changes in national boundaries in Western Europe, the old order was completely changed in the east. The Austro-Hungarian Empire was broken up, the eastern borders of Germany were cut back, and Russia temporarily ceased her domination as a result of the Bolshevik Revolution.

These changes enabled Poland to gain its independence as a republic on 11th November 1918. Once borders were agreed with the Russians in 1921 and other more minor disputes were settled (including the acquisition from Germany of a sizeable portion of the Silesian coalfield by means of a plebiscite in 1921), the new country was able to develop on a sound economic base. For Poland, the export of Silesian coal, especially to the Scandinavian countries, would become a major earner of foreign currency. The Treaty of Versailles gave Poland access to the Baltic around the Bay of Gdansk through the 'free city of Gdansk/Danzig'. However, the Polish Government soon realised that this port was under *de facto* German control, so in 1924 they started building a new port at Gdynia a few miles to the north west on Polish soil. Into this niche developed POLSKAROB: Polsko-Skandynawskie Towarzystwo Transportowe, the Polish-Scandinavian Transport Company.

## ROBUR, POLSKAROB and coal hole leases in Gdynia

One of the major coal mine owners in the Silesian coalfield was Zwiazek Kopaln Gornoslaskich (ROBUR, Union of Upper Silesian Collieries) whose managing director was the engineer Albert Falter. Initially, ROBUR was an investment by the Berlin company EFFCO Emanuel Friedländer and Co., which was associated with the Warburg Bank in Hamburg. On the death of Friedländer the shares in ROBUR were sold in stages to Albert Falter so that by 1936 he became the full owner.

In 1927 the newly-completed coal quay at Gdynia, the Scandinavian Quay, was leased out to Silesian coal companies. Although the Government had recently set up the state shipping company, Żegluga Polska (Polish Steamship Company) it encouraged the coal companies to set up their own shipping companies by offering generous relief in rentals and taxation. However, only ROBUR signed an agreement with the Polish Treasury to build up its own fleet, POLSKAROB, which was to reach 10,000 deadweight tons by 1st May 1929.

An engineer, Napoleon Korzón, was appointed managing director and given a very free hand. For the 585-metre portion of the Scandinavian Quay leased to ROBUR, Korzón immediately ordered a rail-mounted, moveable, coal-truck tippler and loader from Demag of Duisburg. This could lift a 20-ton railway truck and tip its contents directly into a ship's hold, and was the first of its type in Europe. There were also four seven-ton capacity grab cranes. With this modern equipment loading rates of over 400 tons per hour could be achieved, enabling most colliers to be turned round within 12 hours.

### The ROBUR fleet develops

In August 1927 *Ragni*, an elderly Norwegian collier, was purchased by the subsidiary Rederi-och Transport Akt. ROBUR, renamed *Robur* and placed under the Swedish flag. POLSKAROB appointed the Swedish representative of both Friedlander and ROBUR, Wilhelm Römstrom, as shipping consultant. In return for placing *Robur* under the Swedish flag, the Swedish Government opened a consulate in Gdynia with Napoleon Korzón as the honorary consul.

Under her Swedish captain and chief engineer, this ageing collier made a perfect training

*Robur I* as *Robur* when under the Swedish flag between August 1927 and May 1928. She was a typical raised-quarterdeck British-built collier of the late 19th century with two holds forward and one aft. *[Bohdan Huras collection]*

vessel for the new Polish officers and seamen, as her old hull and engines provided plenty of practical experience of engineering and navigation. In May 1928 *Robur* was transferred to the parent company POLSKAROB, renamed *Robur I* and put under the Polish flag. Her service with POLSKAROB was short for in July 1930 she was sold for further trading.

Technically, the first purchase by POLSKAROB was the British collier *Corbrook* on 7th July 1927. She was renamed *Robur II* but, because on purchase less than three-quarters of the crew were Polish, the Polish consulate in London refused temporary registration and for three months she sailed under the Swedish flag, eventually hoisting the Polish flag on 7th October 1927. Service for POLSKAROB was again short. After delivering coal from Gdansk to the northern Swedish port of Piteå, *Robur II* departed light in a north-easterly blizzard on 18th November 1928 with help from the local icebreaker. Once clear of the coast a southerly course was set and she sailed blindly, parallel to the shore. But a combination of an onshore wind pressing on her high, empty hull and local magnetic abnormalities took her off course, and at midnight during a break in the weather she was only one mile from the Bjuroklubb Lighthouse and heading straight towards it. After a sharp turn to port she started to regain the open sea but struck a submerged offshore reef. The after end of the shaft tunnel became impaled on the rocks and she slowly filled with water. In such a remote area the crew's attempts to draw attention to their plight failed and they endured a very

*Robur II* on a lay-by berth at Gdansk-Danzig. Although 30 years younger than *Robur I*, this British-built collier is very similar, though very slightly larger and with an enclosed wheelhouse for the Baltic and a white spirket plate on the bow. *[Bohdan Huras collection]*

uncomfortable stormy night. By dawn on 19th November a change in wind direction enabled all 19 to reach the shore in a boat. They found shelter in a woodcutter's bothy which, though unmanned, was stocked with emergency provisions. About 11.30 am that morning *Robur II* finally settled by the stern, capsized to starboard, and sank.

In order to fulfil its contractual agreements with the Government - 5,000 and 10,000 deadweight tons by 1928 and 1930 respectively - POLSKAROB put four vessels into service over the next two years. In August 1928 the British collier *Akenside* was chartered and, being found economic and efficient, was purchased outright in September 1928 and renamed *Robur III*. In April 1929, on the advice of Wilhelm Römstrom, POLSKAROB ordered two new colliers from Lindholmens-Motala, Gothenburg, Sweden. Allocated the names *Robur IV* and *Robur V*, they each cost £28,000. The last purchase of secondhand tonnage came in August 1929 with the British collier *Pendennis* which was renamed *Robur VI*. This rather larger collier was used to export Polish coal beyond the Baltic to ports around the North Sea and especially to Eire. Within the year *Robur VI* survived a near-fatal crossing of the North

These two photographs of the British-built *Robur III* show the final development of the raised quarterdeck collier which had accommodation and engines midships, and four holds. The Demag coal-wagon tippler loading gantry was the first of its type in 1927. The picture above shows one of the seven-ton capacity grab cranes on the ROBUR-leased Scandinavian quay at Gdynia/Danzig. Of note are the 20-ton steel-framed and steel-bodied railway trucks which brought the coal over 300 miles away from the mines of Silesia in Southern Poland. Much coal has been spilt on the quay, and a heap awaits trimming on the after deck, above. *[Bohdan Huras collection]*

Sea during a storm of hurricane proportions. Both forecastle cable drums were carried away, one partially unwinding and threatening to foul the propeller. Heavy seas carried away part of the bridge wing, breaking the telegraph and jamming it on 'full astern'. Having stopped, *Robur VI* turned broadside to the sea and before order was restored the poop was swept clean of boats and spare gear, and the doors into the poop accommodation were stove in. Five days and nights after passing the Skaw, *Robur VI* finally reached a British east coast port in a virtually derelict state. An S.O.S. had been sent, but the radio antenna was blown out in mid sentence and Danish shore stations had already reported her loss.

Lindholmens-Motala delivered *Robur IV* and *Robur V* in July and September 1930. These modern, Lentz-compound-engined vessels set new standards of accommodation on the Baltic for their 18-man crews and had a speed of 10 knots on only 10 tons of coal per day. They were fitted with self-trimming holds which was a great advantage considering Polish coal is softer and more brittle than British or German coal. Throughout the depressed years of the 1930s the POLSKAROB fleet achieved a very high level of utilisation.

## Bunkering at Gdynia

Whereas the export of coal was largely controlled by international agreements, the supply of ships' bunkers had no such limitations, and Polish coal was of such quality that it enjoyed a good reputation as bunkers. As such, not just prime coal but mixtures of poorer quality were sold, aided by an honest measurement upon delivery. Gdynia soon gained a reputation, even beyond the Baltic, as a bunkering port.

Initially, the traditional manual method of loading with wicker baskets was employed, but soon the more efficient Hamburg method of using coaling barges allied to specially-modified small tugs was adopted. The bunkering barge of 200-400 tons capacity was moored alongside the ship being bunkered, with the tug to the outside. A portable boom was erected near to the bunkering hatch and a running line was run via the boom to a high-speed steam winch at the stern of the tug. This enabled 100kg wicker baskets to be winched up from the barge on to the deck of the receiving ship. The baskets were tipped into a truck running on a length of temporary track and tipped into the bunkering hatch or, if circumstances permitted, a wooden chute was employed. Although filling the baskets was still done manually, the Hamburg method allowed delivery of up to 20 tons per hour.

POLSKAROB adopted the Hamburg method in spring 1928 and operated it for the next ten years with the help of three tugs which were purchased secondhand from Gdansk: *Vega* (26 tons gross, built 1901 by Eriksberg, Goteborg, Sweden): *Nida* (25 tons gross, built 1906 by J.H.N. Wickhorst, Hamburg, Germany; and *Hala* (32 tons gross, built 1922 by Janssen & Schmilinsky, Hamburg). There were also eight coal barges: *Basia*; *Buba* (1875); *Jola* (1898); *Krysia* (1908); *Ewa* (1909); *Marylka* (1912); *Triczi* (1917); and *Ira* (1919).

On 16th December 1937 the revolutionary self-propelled steam bunkering vessel *Robur VII* came into service, and after 1938 only two tugs, *Nida* and *Hala*, and three barges, *Ira*, *Ewa* and *Krysia*, were needed. *Robur VII* was built by A.F. Smulders, Schiedam, Holland, a builder who specialized in dredgers, and this vessel could be described as a dredger working in reverse. She was powered by a pair of triple-expansion engines which drove an endless chain of tubs, taking coal from shutters at the base of the hopper-shaped hold amidships, through a tunnel to the forepeak of the ship, where the tubs were automatically weighed. The conveyor of tubs then ascended an iron latticework tower, angled at 45 degrees, which was cantilevered over the bows by more than 60 feet to a similar height above sea level, when the tubs were tipped into a crane-controlled chute that delivered the coal directly into the ship's bunkering hatch. A loading rate of up to 300 tons per hour was possible, though in practice the trimmers on the ship being bunkered determined the loading rate. Being self-propelled, *Robur VII* allowed bunkering to take place not only on Gdynia roads but, in good weather, in Gdansk Bay, thereby avoiding port dues, towage, mooring and other fees, and saving in time. By now POLSKAROB had its own shipbroking, freight broking, and customs clearance office to provide a comprehensive 'mine to user' coal service.

By 1938 two other coal companies had purchased similar, but secondhand, vessels: *Skarboferme* was bought by the SKARBOPOL Company and *Progress I* by the PROGRESS Company.

## The largest and last

Ordered in September 1937 from Burntisland Shipbuilding Co. Ltd., *Robur VIII* was the largest and most modern bulk carrier in the pre-Second World War Polish merchant marine. She brought the total deadweight tonnage of the POLSKAROB fleet to 16,315 tons, which qualified them for additional tax concessions from the Polish Government. At the time it was hoped that *Robur VIII* would be the forerunner of a whole class of similar vessels. On 3rd July 1938 *Robur VIII* was dedicated by Father Canon T. Turzynski, the Dean of Gdynia. Afterwards, breakfast was served afloat on the quarterdeck hatches in Gdynia Roads, whilst the complete POLSKAROB fleet sailed past dressed overall in review formation. This included *Robur III, IV, V, VI*, *Robur VII* flying flags from her lattice tower to her tall funnel, the two tugs *Hala* and *Nina* and a number of smaller boats. Sadly, this was to be POLSKAROB's finest hour.

## Second World War: outbreak and breakout

As early as 30th March 1939 the Polish Government made a secret agreement with Polish shipowners, both state and private, that if war was to break out with Germany then the Polish merchant and

*Robur VIII* is seen here cruising in Gdynia Roads on her dedication day, 3rd July 1938. She was the largest collier in the Polish merchant marine and, at that time, one of largest vessels of her type. Only the two colliers of the British Gas, Light and Coke Company, *Mr Therm* (2,974/1936) and *Gasfire* (2,972/1936), exceeded her in size. The guests for the dedication ceremony can be seen assembled on the No. 2 hold hatches ahead of the bridge. On the quarterdeck a furled awning has been erected over the tables which are laid for the dedication breakfast, and the partly-raised landing companionway is enclosed in white canvas. *[Bohdan Huras collection]*

naval fleets would attempt to break out from the Baltic and ally themselves with the British merchant and Royal Navies. The merchant fleet would come under the direct control of the Minister of Trade and Industry of the Polish Government in Exile.

At 18.00 hours on 30th August 1939 a signal, which translates as 'Katie and Maria have gone to the forest to pick berries', was broadcast to all Polish ships. It meant 'proceed immediately to Newcastle-on-Tyne or to the nearest neutral port'. At the time *Robur III* was at Methil and *Robur V* was in the Tyne, whilst *Robur VIII* turned around in the North Sea and made for Burntisland. But *Robur VI*, which had arrived that day at Amsterdam and had started unloading, was arrested on the orders of the German consul, who was acting on behalf of an employee of ROBUR who was a German citizen. Although the Polish consul could not help when Captain Zygmunt Kinast asked him to intercede, an appeal to the British consul succeeded. The arrest was lifted, unloading finished, and *Robur VI* left Amsterdam for Methil. Only *Robur IV* was in the Baltic: she was off Gotland heading for Gdynia but she immediately changed course to pass close to Bornholm, passing Copenhagen at 21.00 hours on 31st August. Next morning, whilst running down the Swedish side of the Sound, she was approaching Skagen when a squadron of German destroyers were sighted inbound from the North Sea. *Robur VI's* safety valves were screwed down and, sailing at 12 knots, she just made the shelter of Swedish waters - the Germans respecting Swedish neutrality on the first day of the war. In Gothenberg *Robur IV* joined the Bałtycka Spółka Okrętowa's *Kromań* (1,864/1912) and *Narocz* (1,795/1915), and Żegluga Polska's *Wilno* (2,018/1928) and *Chorzów* (845/1921). Between them they embarked the crew and cadets off the Polish sail training ship, *Dar Pomorza* (1,561/1909) which was interned in Stockholm. Eventually, the convoy sailed coastwise to Bergen in Norway escorted by a Norwegian torpedo boat. Although shadowed by German torpedo boats, their neutrality was respected. On 14th October the five Polish ships, together with a French tanker and a Greek freighter, sailed in convoy to the Firth of Forth escorted by a Royal Navy cruiser and four destroyers. Whilst the *Robur VI* was in Swedish waters, Alfred Falter attempted to transfer her to a Swedish subsidiary. He later became Under-Secretary of State in the Ministry of Finance, Trade and Industry in General Sikorski's Government in Exile in Angers in France.

Only *Robur VII*, the bunkering vessel, was left in Gdynia. She survived the initial bombing but on the night of 6-7th September was scuttled, along with a Greek steamer, to block the main entrance to Gdynia and deny the Germans use of the port.

With very few exceptions most of the Polish merchant fleet and a good proportion of the Polish Navy succeeded in joining the Allies. *Robur VIII* was sent to Liverpool to load supplies for Poland via Roumania, but with the fall of Poland this operation was abandoned. The POLSKAROB board agreed that the ROBUR fleet come under the management of William Cory and Son Ltd., and the ships became a part of the British coastal collier fleet.

## Reorganisation and renaming

To reflect the situation on the ground, in March-April 1940 the ownership of POLSKAROB was changed, Alfred Falter becoming owner with his headquarters in Angers, France but with the ships retaining the Polish flag and Gdynia registry. The main reason for this was that both ROBUR the coal owning company and POLSKAROB still had German connections, as was demonstrated by *Robur VI's* detention in Amsterdam. From April 1940 *Robur III* became *Kmicic*, *Robur IV* became *Częstochowa*, *Robur V* became *Kordecki*, *Robur VI* became *Zbaraż* and *Robur VIII* became *Zagloba*.

Within a few weeks *Kmicic* under Captain Adam Fiedorowicz found herself in the thick of the action. Having arrived in Bordeaux on 6th June with a cargo of groundnuts from Africa, her unloading was protracted due to the situation just prior to the fall of France. The smaller Żegluga Polska vessel *Chorzów* was also in Bordeaux. Some of the retreating Polish forces in France made for Bordeaux and on the night of 18th June the *Chorzów* got away after General Sikorski had intervened with Admiral Darlan, carrying over 200 Polish evacuees and the Wawel jewels from the Polish Crown castle in Krakow. Polish refugees now made for the *Kmicic*. With capitulation in mind, the port authorities prevented the *Kmicic* from sailing, enforced on 21st June by a force of Gendarmerie. However, at about 17.00 hours a detachment of well-armed Polish Highlanders arrived and nullified the guard on the ship. That evening *Kmicic* was locked out, sailing with over 500 refugees including a valuable 'cargo' of Polish and Czech airmen. Passage was made down the Gironde in the dark with no information as to minefields. By now the Germans were entering Bordeaux. *Kmicic* anchored in Le Verdon Roads, managing to avoid the attention of German aircraft, but the expected convoy for England did not materialise. Eventually she sailed alone to Falmouth at 11 to 12 knots delivering her priceless cargo of airmen, many of whom then took part in the Battle of Britain.

With the fall of France, the Polish Government in Exile transferred to London whilst Alfred Falter set up his headquarters in New York.

## War losses

During the war most of Alfred Falter's fleet was employed in the North Sea coal trade. On 15th July 1940 *Zbaraż* (ex-*Robur VII*) was running light in convoy northwards when at 14.30 hours about 10 miles south of the Aldeburgh Light Vessel the convoy was bombed by German aircraft. Although *Zbaraż* was not directly hit, the concussion damaged her machinery and started leaks in the aftermost hold. *Zbaraż* was towed towards Harwich but after two hours the non-essential crew members were taken off and about 12 miles off Harwich, near the South Ship Head Buoy, her stern touched bottom and she stuck fast, despite the efforts of two tugs. *Zbaraż* was abandoned just before midnight and sank on 16th July. Her crew was rescued.

The *Częstochowa* (ex-*Robur IV*) also had a short but eventful war. In February 1940 when near to her destination of Sunderland she was nearly lost when she was overtaken by a severe storm which threatened to blow her empty bulk ashore. The only way to save her was to try and enter the port of Sunderland at night, although it was protected by a boom. Fortunately, she was recognized and the barrage opened just in time to save her from damage. On 12th September 1940 she sailed from Methil to Canada in a convoy which included the ill-fated *City of Benares* (11,081/1936). Arriving on 25th September in the Gulf of St. Lawrence, she took a month to load a full cargo of woodpulp. The return journey began on 24th October and for part of the way the escort included the Polish destroyer ORP *Garland*. When in Canada the ship was visited by Napoleon Korzón who expressed his wish that the Falter fleet operate coastwise on the American eastern seaboard. The British authorities would not agree to this and she was time chartered by the Ministry of War Transport back into the east coast coal trade. Almost a year later, loaded with cement for Reykjavik, *Czestochowa* was in a northbound convoy when she was attacked by German S-boats off Sheringham on the night of 19-20th September 1941. *S-48* had damaged the France, Fenwick collier *Dalewood* (2,774/1931) and with two torpedoes blew off the bows of the *Czestochowa*. The cargo of cement partly muffled the torpedoes as the collier was crossing a sandbank near the Sheringham Buoy and she drove under, breaking in two abaft the bridge. Most of the crew manned the boats on the poop and rescued three others, including the captain who was standing up to his chest in water on the monkey island. The survivors were transferred to escorting motor gun boats and after an hour or two all but one of the missing men were found. Only the third officer was lost, being overwhelmed in his cabin beneath the bridge.

In August 1940 the *Zagloba* (ex-*Robur VIII*) was put into Atlantic convoys as a general cargo carrier, and in two-and-a-half years had completed 19 round trips. Her twentieth voyage saw her loading military supplies in New York. She departed at the end of January 1943 in convoy SC 118, one of largest comprising 64 ships and 10 escorts. The convoy was attacked by 20 U-boats and 18 ships were lost, including *Zagloba*, for the loss of three attackers. The exact fate of *Zagloba* remains a matter of conjecture. German sources report that *U 262* attacked three tankers in position 56° 32' north by 16° west at 23.00 hours on 6th February. The first tanker was seen to break apart in 20 minutes, and another was hit but the results were not observed. (A deeply laden collier has a very similar silhouette to a tanker.) However, according to the convoy commodore's ship, the *Zagloba* was seen, with a decided list to port, trying to catch up with the convoy on 9th February. The weather in the North Atlantic was at its worst and it may be that sometime afterwards *Zagloba* was overwhelmed and foundered with the loss of all 28 crew and seven DEMS gunners. Five of the crew and six of the gunners were British, the rest were Polish.

## The surviving ships

The two survivors, *Kordecki* (ex-*Robur V*) and *Kmicic* (ex-*Robur III*), had contrasting war experiences. The former saw little action, whereas *Kmicic* was right in the thick of things. In the early part of the war whilst in a small coastal convoy from Plymouth to the Bristol Channel, the escorting corvette contacted a U-boat off the Lizard and set off in pursuit. The unprotected convoy was then attacked by three Dornier bombers but the Polish crew of *Kmicic* manned the guns and first one and then a second Dornier was hit. Both trailing smoke, the first was seen to crash into the sea, and the second was not presumed to survive. The third flew off after dumping its bombs.

On the night of 3-4th May 1942 *Kmicic*,

The ill-fated *Zagloba*, ex-*Robur VIII*, at New York on 10th October 1942. [US Coast Guard, Eric Johnson collection, courtesy Bill Schell]

loaded with cased aviation spirit, was part of two convoys anchored in the Solent off Cowes when the area received an air raid. As the convoy had been anchored for some time, *Kmicic's* boiler fires were drawn and escape was impossible. That night the crew expended all their ammunition defending the ship, and despite bombs exploding nearby she sustained only moderate damage with one crewman slightly injured. Although she was leaking petrol, *Kmicic* did not catch fire.

In June 1944 *Kmicic* and *Kordecki* were two of the nine Polish merchant ships that took part in Operation Neptune. They sailed from the Bristol Channel as ammunition carriers on 5th June in convoy EBC 2Z to the Omaha and Utah beachheads for the American part of the invasion of Normandy, arriving there on 8th June. Their convoy was accompanied by the Żegluga Polska's *Katowice* (1,995/1925) and *Kraków* (2,017/1926). Soon after the liberation of Ghent by the Polish First Armoured Division, *Kmicic* - laden with supplies - became the first Allied ship to traverse the Ghent canal and enter the port of Ghent on 20th December 1944.

## Post-war decline and fall

Although the Allies won the Second World War, Poland lost out: she merely exchanged Nazi domination for Soviet domination. The new communist government placed coal mines and shipping companies under non-compensatory state ownership. It therefore comes as no surprise that Alfred Falter did not return to Poland. If his ships had returned they would have been put into the Polska Żegluga Morska (PŻM) fleet. The POLSKAROB coal loading facilities at Gdynia had been destroyed in May 1945 by the Germans as they retreated before the Red Army.

November 1946 saw Alfred Falter retaining his New York headquarters whilst his two ships were re-registered in Panama. The *Kmicic* was renamed *Chopin* and *Kordecki* became *Copernicus*. Both retained their Polish captains and crew and operated in the Mediterranean, North Africa and around Spain with general cargoes. Alfred Falter was a generous shipowner, paying a thirteenth month's salary at Christmas and giving the officers a premium on the cargo they carried. He was repaid by very loyal and hardworking crews. Unfortunately, this Indian Summer was to prove short-lived. In 1948 the *Chopin* was sold to other Panamanian owners.

Partly from the proceeds of this sale, Alfred Falter ordered a new motor tramp ship from William Pickersgill and Sons Ltd., which was completed in July 1949 as the *Alfa* and placed under the Liberian flag. Her entry into service led in 1949 to the sale of the *Copernicus* to Belgian owners. In 1952 Alfred Falter withdrew from shipowning by selling *Alfa* to Norwegian owners. But it was not until 28th May 1966, 27 years after the POLSKAROB Company ceased trading in Poland, that an ordinary general meeting of the shareholders agreed to put the company into liquidation.

## Salvaged to become a salvor

The bunkering vessel *Robur VII*, which was scuttled as a block ship at the main entrance to the port of Gdynia, was raised within a few months by the Germans and in 1942 converted into a salvage vessel by Vulcan Stettiner Maschinenbau A.G., Stettin, to be renamed *Richard*. Her tower was cut away and the bunkering equipment removed. The hold was converted into workshops and stores, whilst living accommodation was provided in a substantial block under the navigation bridge, which had been raised. Two derricks were built on the strengthened deck together with all the salvage bitts and attachments. The Germans put *Richard* to work in Norwegian waters until the end of the war. On 12th December

*Copernicus*, formerly *Kordecki* and before that *Robur V*, off Penarth Head in 1948. *[Welsh Industrial and Maritime Museum Hansen Collection 2085/2148]*

1945 she was ceded to Great Britain and sent to Methil. Under the terms of the division of the German fleet, however, Britain transferred the vessel to the U.S.S.R. where, under the name *Khosta*, she operated as a naval auxiliary during 1946 and 1947. Meanwhile, however, the Polish Sea Mission in Hamburg and a department of the Polish Office of Maritime Affairs were searching for the old *Robur VII*. Having proved Poland's claim of ownership to the Russian Government, *Khosta* was handed over to the Towing and Salvage Division of Żegluga Polska on 14th April 1947 at Swinoujscie and renamed *Smok*. In post-war years *Smok* assisted the salvage of several hundred wartime wrecks off the Polish coast including, in 1951, the raising of the German battleship *Gneisenau* which was blocking the main entrance to Gdynia and, in 1954, the salvage of the German transport *Seeburg* off Jastarnia. Almost completed before the war by Burmeister and Wain, Copenhagen as the *Adelaide Star* (11,000/1940) for Blue Star Line, she had been seized by the Germans (see *Record* 9). Attending less and less arduous tasks as the years went by, *Smok* was sold for scrap in 1990, bringing to a close the history of POLSKAROB.

# POLSKAROB Polsko Skandynawskie Towarzystwo Transportowe S. A.
## Alfred Falter
## Gdynia

### 1. ROBUR/ROBUR I  1927-1930  Iron
975g  577n  220.4 x 29.7 x 16.7 feet
C. 2-cyl. by Hall, Russell and Co., Aberdeen; 98 NHP, 7 knots.
*10.1879:* Launched by Hall, Russell and Co., Aberdeen (Yard No.214) for J. and A. Davidson, Aberdeen as BALLOGIE.
*1884:* Sold to Fisher, Renwick and Co., Newcastle and renamed KATE FORSTER.
*1895:* Sold to Dampskibsselskabet 'Ragni' (Erling Lund, manager), Christiania, Norway and renamed RAGNI.
*1901:* Owner became Dampskibacties Ragni (Erling Lund, manager), Christiania.
*1917:* Taken over by The Shipping Controller (Temple, Thompson and Clark, managers), London.
*1919:* Returned to Dampskibacties Ragni (Erling Lund, manager), Oslo.
*1926:* Sold to Erling Mortensen, Oslo, Norway.
*8.1927:* Sold to Rederi-och Transport Akt. Robur (W. Ronström Senior, manager), Stockholm, Sweden and renamed ROBUR.

*5.1928:* Acquired by POLSKAROB Polsko Skandynawskie Towarzystwo Transportowe S.A., Gdynia, Poland and renamed ROBUR I.
*7.1930:* Sold to Rederi A/B Rewa, Stockholm, Sweden and renamed REWA.
*7.1934:* Sold for breaking up to Marine Yard, Libau (Liepaja), Latvia.

### 2. ROBUR II  1927-1928
1,370g  797n  2050d  235.0 x 36.1 x 15.6 feet.
T.3-cyl. by George Clark Ltd., Sunderland; 180 NHP.
*11.12.1909:* Launched by S. P. Austin and Son Ltd., Sunderland (Yard No. 252) for William Cory and Son Ltd., London as DEVEREUX.
*1.1910:* Completed.
*16.4.1916:* Owners became Cory Colliers Ltd.
*1920:* Renamed CORBROOK.
*1927:* Sold to Samuel P. Jackson, Grangemouth.
*7.7.1927:* Acquired by POLSKAROB Polsko Skandynawskie Towarzystwo Transportowe S. A., Gdynia, Poland, and renamed ROBUR II under the Swedish flag.
*7.10.1927:* Registered in Poland.
*18.11.1928:* Whilst on a voyage from Piteå to Gdynia in ballast ran onto rocks near Bjuroklubb Lighthouse in position 64.19 north, 21.29 east. She was abandoned by her crew and sank the next day.

### 3. ROBUR III/KMICIC/CHOPIN  1928-1948
1,894g  1,138n  2,895d  264.0 x 39.0 x 17.0 feet
T. 3-cyl. by George Clark Ltd., Sunderland; 215 NHP, 1,060 IHP, 10 knots.
*19.3.1923:* Launched by Robert Thompson and Sons Ltd., Sunderland (Yard No. 317).
*4.1923:* Completed.
*16.4.1923:* Registered in the ownership of the Quayside Shipping Co. Ltd. (Connell and Grace Ltd., managers), Newcastle-upon-Tyne as AKENSIDE.
*9.1928:* Acquired by POLSKAROB Polsko Skandynawskie Towarzystwo Transportowe S.A., Gdynia, Poland and renamed ROBUR III.
*4.1940:* Owner became Alfred Falter, Angers, France (William Cory and Son Ltd., London, manager) and renamed KMICIC remaining registered in Poland.
*11.1946:* Owner became Alfred Falter, New York, USA and renamed CHOPIN under the Panama flag.
*1948:* Sold to Compania Naviera Audax S.A., Panama and renamed ESPERANZA.
*1949:* Sold to Sebastiano Tuillier, Venice, Italy.
*1955:* Sold to Paolo Tomei, Genoa, Italy and renamed DANIELA T.
*3.1960:* Broken up at Trieste by SIDEMAR.

*Chopin*, ex- *Robur III* and *Kmicic*, at Cardiff on 12th January 1948.
*[Welsh Industrial and Maritime Museum Hansen Collection 1876/1953]*

*Robur VI, seen here loading at the Scandinavian Quay, Gdynia using the seven-ton grab cranes, was built in Holland to the modern British collier design of four holds, bridge amidships, engine aft, and a raised quarterdeck. Her masting is unusual with a single derrick servicing holds ahead and abaft the bridge from the fore- and main-masts. The fore hold was served by a single derrick on a sampson post and a similar arrangement was used for the after hold. Robur VI was the only vessel in the fleet with white edging to her hull. [Bohdan Huras collection]*

## 4. ROBUR VI/ZBARAZ 1929-1940

2,088g 1,252n 3,200d 275.5 x 40.2 x 17.2 feet.
T. 3-cyl. by N.V. Maschinenbau, Bolnes, Holland; 249 NHP, 1,250 IHP, 9 knots.
*1.1922*: Completed by Jonker & Stans, Hendrik Ido Ambacht (Yard No.147) for Bureau Wijsmuller, Den Haag, Holland as STRAAT SOENDA.
*1922*: Stranded on Kiskola Reef in the Gulf of Finland, and aground for ten days.
*1.1924*: Sold to Pendennis Steam Ship Co. Ltd. (Wilson and Armstrong, managers), Newcastle-upon-Tyne and renamed PENDENNIS.
*8.1929*: Acquired by POLSKAROB Polsko Skandynawskie Towarzystwo Transportowe S.A., Gdynia, Poland and renamed ROBUR VI.
*1940*: Owner became Alfred Falter, Angers, France (William Cory and Son Ltd., London, managers) and renamed ZBARAŻ, remaining registered in Poland.
*15.7.1940*: Damaged by German aircraft 10 miles south of the Aldeburgh Light Vessel whilst on a voyage from London to

Hartlepool in ballast. Taken in tow first by one of the convoy escorts and later a tug but capsized and sank in position 51.53.48 north, 01.34.24 east near the South Ship Head Buoy, about 12 miles from Harwich.

## 5. ROBUR IV/CZESTOCHOWA 1930-1941

1,971g 1,067n 2,960d 257.3 x 41.1 x 18.8 feet.
C.4-cyl. by Akt. Lindholmen-Motala, Gothenburg, Sweden;145 NHP; 10 knots.
*7.1930*: Completed by Akt. Lindholmen-Motala, Gothenburg, Sweden (Yard No. 932), for POLSKAROB Polsko Skandynawskie Towarzystwo Transportowe S. A., Gdynia, Poland as ROBUR IV.
*1940*: Owner became Alfred Falter, Angers, France (William Cory and Son Ltd., London, managers) and renamed CZESTOCHOWA, remaining registered in Poland.
*20.8.1941*: Sank after being torpedoed by the German torpedo boat S 48 near Sheringham Buoy in position 53.11 north, 01.06 east whilst on a voyage from London via the Tyne to Reykjavik with a cargo of cement. One member of her crew was lost.

*Robur IV, like her sister Robur V, was a Swedish-built collier. Her extensive accommodation amidships and aft together with wing cabs fit her for the Baltic winters. Also of note is the lack of a raised quarterdeck. Her livery was black hull, red boot topping, and white superstructure. The black funnel bore a white diamond on a red band, and within the diamond a white letter R was superimposed on a blue background. [Bohdan Huras collection]*

## 6. ROBUR V/KORDECKI/COPERNICUS   1930-1949

1,975g  1,073n  2,960d  257.6 x 41.1 x 18.6 feet.

C.4-cyl. by Akt. Lindholmen-Motala, Gothenburg, Sweden;145 NHP; 10 knots.

*9.1930*: Completed by Akt. Lindholmen-Motala, Gothenburg, Sweden (Yard No. 933) for POLSKAROB Polsko Skandynawskie Towarzystwo Transportowe S. A., Gdynia, Poland as ROBUR V.

*1940*: Owner became Alfred Falter, Angers, France (William Cory and Son Ltd., London, managers) and renamed KORDECKI, remaining registered in Poland.

*11.1946*: Owner became Alfred Falter, New York, USA and renamed COPERNICUS under the Panama flag.

*1949*: Sold to Marcel Goossens, Liége, Belgium and renamed SUZON.

*10.1950*: Sold to Bernhard Blumenfeld GmbH, (Reederei Blumenfeld GmbH, managers), Hamburg, West Germany.

*18.11.1950*: Renamed BERNHARD BLUMENFELD.

*11.1954*: Sold to Erich Ahrens, Hamburg.

*22.4.1955*: Renamed INGEBORG AHRENS.

*10.1956*: Sold to Partenreederei "Saxonia" (Werner Peters, manager), Hamburg.

*19.1.1957*: Renamed SAXONIA.

*1.2.1960*: Sold to Pietro Belachi, Ravenna, Italy, and renamed CLASSIS.

*1963*: Owner became Societa Romagnola d'Armamento, Cesenatico, Italy (Pietro Belacchi, Ravenna, Italy, manager).

*1966*: Owner became Compania de Navegacion Celestemar S. A., Panama (Pietro Belacchi, Ravenna, manager) and renamed ATSI.

*25.5.1968*: Brodospas commenced demolition at Split, Yugoslavia.

## 7. ROBUR VII   1937-1939

895g  441n  1,200d  169.3 x 42.1 x 17.8 feet (184.6 overall, 244.5 including elevator)

Two x T. 3-cyl. by N.V. Werf Gusto v.h. A.F. Smulders, Schiedam, Holland driving twin screws; 750 IHP, 6 knots.

*4.10.1937*: Launched by N.V. Werf Gusto v.h. A.F. Smulders, Schiedam, Holland (Yard No. 722).

*16.12.1937*: Completed for POLSKAROB Polsko Skandynawskie Towarzystwo Transportowe S. A., Gdynia, Poland as ROBUR VII.

*7.9.1939*: Scuttled at the entrance to the port of Gdynia as a block ship.

*1939*: Raised by Germans, owners became Deutsches Reich-Treuhandstelle Ost Seeschiff, Danzig, Germany (Eisen und Metall A.G., Hamburg, Germany, managers).

*1940*: Renamed RICHARD.

*15.11.1940*: Sold to Eisen und Metall A.G., Hamburg.

*24.7.1942*: Re-registered after conversion into a salvage vessel by Vulcan Stettiner Maschinenbau AG, Stettin, Germany.

*12.12.1945*: Arrived at Methil.

*1946*: Allocated to the USSR, operated as a naval auxiliary and renamed KHOSTA.

*14.4.1947*: Returned to Wydział Holowniczo Ratowniczy (Towing and Salvage Division of ZBARAŻ Polska), Gdynia and renamed SMOK.

*1.1.1951*: Owners became Polskie Ratownictwo Okretowe (Polish Ship Salvage Company), Gdynia.

*4.1990*: Sold for breaking up.

*10.6.1990*: Breaking up began by Recuperaciones Siderurgicas y Navales at Maliano, Cantabria, Spain.

*Robur V* had a long life after Falter sold her as *Copernicus* in 1949. She is seen, right as *Robur V* and below as *Saxonia*. [Right: Captain J.F. van Puyvelde/A. Duncan; below: Rolf Meinecke, courtesy Gert Uwe Detlefsen]

## 8. ROBUR VIII/ZAGLOBA 1938-1943

2,864g 1,611n 4,300d 313.7 x 44.5 x 19.7 feet.
T.3-cyl. by North Eastern Marine Engineering Co. Ltd., Sunderland; 244 NHP, 1,200 IHP; 9 knots.
*30.4.1938*: Launched by the Burntisland Ship Building Co. Ltd., Burntisland, (Yard No. 223).
*22.6.1938*: Completed for POLSKAROB Polsko Skandynawskie Towarzystwo Transportowe S. A., Gdynia, Poland as ROBUR VIII.
*1940*: Owner became Alfred Falter, Angers, France (William Cory and Son Ltd., London, managers) and renamed ZAGLOBA, remaining registered in Poland.
*6.2.1943*: Believed to have been sunk by the German submarine U 262 in position 56.32 north, 16.00 west in convoy SC 118 whilst on a voyage from New York and St. John, Newfoundland to Manchester with general cargo. It is also possible that she foundered in heavy weather a few days later. All 28 of the crew and seven DEMS gunners were lost.

# Alfred Falter, New York

## 9. ALFA 1949-1952

2,808g 1,345n 4,600d 332.1 x 48.3 x 19.8 feet
Oil engine 6-cyl. 2SCSA by J.G. Kincaid and Co. Ltd., Greenock; 427 NHP, 1,800 BHP.

*14.4.1949*: Launched by William Pickersgill and Sons Ltd., Sunderland (Yard No. 317).
*7.1949*: Completed for Alfred Falter, New York, USA as ALFA under the Liberian flag.
*1952*: Sold to Skibs A/S Skibsfart (Jac Salvesen, manager), Farsund, Norway and renamed NORMUNDO.
*1956*: Renamed WILLMAR.
*1963*: Sold to Skibs A/S Bodin (Jacob Sannes and Co., managers), Bodø, Norway and renamed BODIN.
*28.5.1966*: Caught fire following an explosion in the engine room in the River Scheldt during a voyage from Charleston to Hamburg with a cargo of paper and chemicals. Beached at Fort Filip.
*2.6.1966*: Refloated but later declared a constructive total loss.
*1966*: Sold to Frangmouge Compania Naviera S.A., Panama (George Moundreas and Brothers S.A., Piraeus, Greece, managers), repaired and renamed GOOD HOPE under the Greek flag.
*1973*: Sold to Unimax Shipping Panama S.A., Panama (Leandros Shipping Co S.A., Piraeus, Greece, managers) and renamed PANGRI under the Greek flag.
*1976*: Sold to A.S. Trader Maritime Co., Limassol, Cyprus (Golden Fleet Navigation Co. S.A., Piraeus, Greece, managers), and renamed AGNI under the Cypriot flag.
*4.8.1977*: Arrived at Gadani Beach, Pakistan to be broken up.

Alfred Falter's *Alfa*, registered in Monrovia, Liberia, is seen berthed at New York (top of page). When Alfred Falter withdrew from shipowning in 1952, *Alfa* was sold to Jac Salvesen of Farsund and later carried the name *Willmar* (right).

*Dominic* running for Lamport and Holt, with their funnel colours and the poop and forecastle in 'Lamport black'. *[Fotoflite incorporating Skyfotos]*

# DOMINIC AND HER BRAZILIAN CREW
## Captain A.W. Kinghorn

During my five year's cadetship - two years aboard HMS *Conway* followed by three years in the Blue Star Line of London - I had been shipmates with British crews exclusively, except for the occasional refugee from the Baltic states who had adopted British nationality. *Conway* boys came from all over the British Isles. Even though most deepsea Blue Star crews signed on in either London or Liverpool, men also came from other southern ports, many more from Merseyside, while Welshmen and Irishmen also used 'La'Pool' as their port of origin. Others came from the north east coast and England's south west. There was always a solid nucleus of men from Scotland and the Outer Hebrides. The main attraction for the ratings was the overtime pay, which was good - and many hands remained for years in Blue Star ships. By the time I obtained my second mate's certificate in October 1954 I was pretty well versed in most of the divers British dialects, which helped overcome future language barriers.

**Too good to refuse**

Returning to the Blue Star fold after a month's leave I was sent relieving third mate in London's Royal Docks aboard the *Uruguay Star* (10,723/1948) for five days, then for two days aboard the *Tasmania Star* (11,950/1950). With British crews. In London my job entailed - with other mates and cadets - keeping check on the unloading and loading of cargo, supervising the taking aboard of deck stores for the forthcoming voyage, attending surveys on the lifeboats and other lifesaving equipment, making and checking crew lists and emergency drill muster lists, and helping calculate harbour wages. There was usually time in the evenings to go ashore, or visit old friends aboard other ships with which the Royal Docks were always crowded. Then, on the morning of 7th December I was summoned from the '*Tazzy*' lying at 'D' shed, Royal Victoria Dock, through pouring rain to the Blue Star Line office at 'B' berth, where I was asked by Captain 'Sam' Dickers, the Marine Superintendent, if I would like to sail that evening for the Amazon in the Booth Line *Dominic* - '*Nothing like the 12,000 tons of the* Tasmania Star*, Mr Kinghorn, but you'd sail as second mate.*'

The assistant superintendent standing behind him immediately made 'don't go!' signals, but the rank of second mate at age 21 was unheard of in Blue Star. Too tempting an offer to refuse. I was aware that Booth Line and Lamport and Holt had been absorbed into the Vestey empire after the Second World War. Although they continued to run their own ships under their own colours with their own office and seafaring staff, Booth Line were suddenly short of a second mate, and Captain Dickers had been asked to help. '*I hope you can speak Portuguese!*' said his assistant

laconically. I couldn't. I had a little Spanish but, as was pointed out, Portuguese is different.

When the taxi deposited me on the quayside at 12 Shed, King George V Dock I found I was looking, not up at the kind of ship I was used to, but down upon a narrow maindeck. Hatches battened down, she was ready for sea, needing only a couple more officers. It was still raining and the short December afternoon nearly over when several gloomy-looking oilskinned sailors silently appeared and carried aboard my tin seatrunk, canvas seabag, and suitcase. It took me several days at sea to realise they were not Portuguese at all, only speaking it, and that their home town was Belem, in the Amazon. Men from Brazil.

The second mate I was relieving was a much older man. '*Are you bloody mad?*' he barked, when I introduced myself. '*I hope not,*' I replied, somewhat abashed. '*Well you soon ****** will be on this ****** ship,*' he said, and without further ado he departed, reeking of whisky. He left me no handover notes: I was 'in at the deep end'. The new mate was a Welshman in his middle forties, while the new third mate was 19 years old, a Lamport and Holt cadet who, like me, had been 'asked to come'. Between Captain Roberts and the mate, and us two youngsters, there yawned a generation gap - 25 years - the effects of which were to last throughout the six-and-a-half month voyage. The chief engineer, Mr Watson, was a nice old boy from Glasgow, and the other officers, all British, were mostly on our side of middle-age. The Brazilians, too, were mostly youngish men, though the bosun, in his forties, was deemed quite elderly. There were no cadets. Total complement was 35.

The ship had loaded a full general cargo in London for La Guira and Puerto La Cruz, both in Venezuela; Willemstad in Curacao; Cartagena in Colombia; and Belem, Sao Luiz de Maranho and Fortaleza, all in north Brazil. We occasionally carried up to six passengers. In those days Lamport and Holt traded from Liverpool to the Brazil south of Pernambuco (Recife), while Booth Line ran to north Brazil, including the Amazon. Both companies also ran services between Brazil and New York.

My first watch at sea - the midnight to 4.00 am middle watch - had us heading into a freshening westerly in the English Channel and making, I perceived, the magnificent speed of four knots. As the weather improved over the following weeks we hurtled along at 12 knots on a good day: about the same speed as my previous *Saxon Star* (7,355/1942) and many other war-built ships.

That first night out, once we had disembarked our pilot off Dungeness, Captain Roberts studied the dark horizon all around, remarked that there were few ships likely to close us, and left me to it. A rough sea, rising westerly swell, ship in automatic steering. With me - one Brazilian sailor on watch keeping lookout, and who would take the steering if necessary. Before ships were routed in the Channel you steered as directly as possible for your destination, keeping a good lookout and altering course 'in sufficient time to prevent collision'. I found my watchmate spoke no English, but made excellent strong black coffee. As few of our Brazilians spoke any English I realised I had to acquire a smattering of Portuguese, rapidly!

Next afternoon a white-painted homeward-bound banana-laden ship bearing a familiar funnel passed up channel. She was the recently-acquired *Albion Star* (3,022/1939), soon to be transferred to Lamport and Holt as *Balzac*. One of several ships which underwent a rather bewildering succession of name and funnel changes, she followed a practice which enabled Blue Star, Lamport and Holt, and Booth Line to run a pool of ships retaining individual identities in their various trades. Originally the Norwegian MOSDALE, her subsequent Vestey names of *Carroll*, *Norman Star*, and *Basil* typified this arrangement. Sold to Greeks in 1964, she was not scrapped until 1973, her 34 years standing testimony to her builders, Burmeister and Wain of Copenhagen.

## Getting to know *Dominic*

The *Dominic*, a mere 3,860 tons gross, was indeed much smaller than my previous ships. Her length of 323.9 feet between perpendiculars required her to carry overside not only the usual load lines but the Winter North Atlantic (WNA) loadline, mandatory for vessels under 330 feet in length. Yet, once I got used to her, she seemed large enough.

Built in 1945 in Wilmington, California by the Consolidated Steel Corporation as the *Hickory Stream* for the U.S. Maritime Commission (USMC), she and her numerous sisters were intended for an assault which never took place - the final seaborne attack on Japan which the 1945 surrender fortunately rendered unnecessary. Post-war many were retained by the USMC, but others found their way into the merchant fleets of many nations. This included *Dominic*, which went to Booth Line in 1947.

Lacking radar - like many ships at that time - *Dominic* nevertheless had the latest Sperry gyro compass, with auto-steering and valve follow-up which was a great improvement on the older trolley/contactor model. Throughout my cadetship I had never even seen a gyro compass, let alone found myself in charge of one, but fortunately the Welsh mate came to my rescue and showed me how to start it before we sailed from London. Thereafter I studied the instruction manual assiduously. There was also an echo sounder, brass-labelled by its US manufacturer as a 'supersonic depth indicator'.

Built with accommodation and engines aft, *Dominic's* layout resembled one of today's ships rather than one of 1945 vintage. A raised forecastle housed cargo space and the windlass contactor room, carpenter's workshop, and lamproom, abaft which were three large cargo hatches with single 'tween decks and steel pontoon covers, tarpaulins secured overall with steel battens and wooden wedges. Two masts between the hatches carried fidded topmasts and, on the fore, a small topgallant mast. This was unusual, as were the topmasts carrying radio aerials on both sampson posts at the forward corners of the bridge. The three big hatches were served by ten union-purchase 10-ton SWL derricks with two heavy derricks amidships, originally for handling tanks and other weighty military equipment. Abaft the accommodation on the poop was the small number 4 hold and two 'tweendeck refrigerated cargo chambers for military provisions. This hatch was served by a pair of SWL 1.25-ton beautifully varnished wooden derricks: the bosun's pride and joy.

Two big steel lifeboats hung in gravity davits (another first for yours truly whose previous ships carried their wooden boats under luffing davits). Unlike most US-built ships of that era she was not a steamship: propulsion was supplied by a six-cylinder Nordberg oil engine manufactured in Milwaukee, Wisconsin and typifying the massive nationwide war effort the Americans were making in 1945. Accommodation fittings such as bunks, chairs, and desks were all of steel and painted battleship grey, while cabin 'carpets' were luxurious coco matting. It was all pretty basic, but comfortable when you got used to it.

*Albion Star.* Blue Star name, but Lamport and Holt colours.

Inside entry to the bridge was up a wide steel staircase through a trapdoor into the chartroom. The forepart of the bridge was in a straight line, port to starboard, with the wheelhouse set back a couple of feet, leaving an outside passage just wide enough to walk through, and instead of rectangular wheelhouse windows there were big round portholes with windscreen wipers. An upper open bridge with steering wheel shaded by a canvas awning was often used by the watchkeepers in fine, warm weather. Although Booth Line had by now painted the house flag on their ships' funnels, *Dominic's* remained plain black. Perhaps it was considered too small and insignificant, crouching, as it were, abaft the tall signal mast.

Captain Roberts RD, RNR had been a midshipman in the Battle of Jutland in 1916. He ran the little *Dominic* kindly, in the grand manner, which suited me as that was what I was used to, and the Brazilians, too, seemed to prefer their ship run smartly. However, some of the other officers were less impressed by the spit and polish.

**Getting to know the Brazilians**

Brazil, I learned, was visited by African voyagers long before 1493, the year Pope Alexander VI divided the Atlantic territories between Spain and Portugal in his famous Bull of Demarcation. Brazil was allocated to Portugal as a colony, while the territories to the south became Spanish. The Portuguese never applied a colour bar and the free intermixing of the races has resulted in the marvellous range of appearances which characterises the Brazilians of today. At first I was inwardly nervous of the Brazilian crew - fear of the unknown. Especially sinister were those with black skins and oriental features. But I need not have worried. Portuguese names such as Silva, Pereira, and de Souza predominated. As the voyage progressed to Venezuela, the West Indies, up and down the north Brazilian coast (as feeder ship to the mainline steamer, *Hilary*, at Belem), up to New York, Norfolk and Newport News, and then back to Brazil I learned that the crew were a highly-versatile crowd. Each seemed perfectly suited to the job of AB (steering the ship, splicing fibre and wire rope, and other 'sailorising' jobs), or of greaser (assisting the engineers in tending the main and auxiliary engines), or of assistant cook/steward. By mutual consent they often switched from deck to engine room to saloon or galley and back again. Often when we arrived in port the cook would come out of his galley to help put out the mooring ropes and tie up the ship. Considering variety to be the spice of life, they were in fact a general purpose crew, way ahead of their time.

The colour of their faces, which at first I found so alarming, was quite forgotten as each man's personality emerged from behind his face. After a week in Belem we sailed one early morning bound for Tutoya Bay. The sailor on watch with me was extremely pensive - by no means his normal, cheery self. When I asked him if all had been well at home he lugubriously told me that 'last night a man was killed in my house. Stabbed by his sweetheart. What a mess'. His 'house' was a brothel, run in his absence by his wife and her brother. This knifing had been the result of a longstanding feud and, whilst not an unusual event, had cast a damper on his last night at home.

The sailors changed watches in rotation each weekend, and the following week's sailor announced to me one fine afternoon, in English, that he neither smoked, drank, nor went with women other than his wife. 'I am very, very good,' he added seriously. In Brazilian ports of course, the lads were on their home ground and the ship's progress was enhanced by their knowing exactly what was what: who ashore had to be listened to, and who must be ignored.

Entering Tutoya Bay between jagged reefs, and also at certain narrow parts of the Amazon, soundings were taken by heaving the hand lead line - the first time I had seen this ancient equipment used in earnest. Captain Roberts explained that the supersonic depth indicator often gave false readings in broken or muddied water, so it was back to basics. 'By the mark, five ...' in Portuguese, of course! Being great fishermen, the crew trailed at least one line from the ship on ocean passages, and at 11 knots plenty of fish including barracuda were caught and soon committed to the pot. They were a cheerful crew, always laughing and joking with each other.

The Brazilian coastal waters were full of interesting shipping. At that time Lloyd Brasileiro owned many vessels and their black hulls and black-topped white funnels were a familiar sight. While some were very modern, more were of amazing antiquity dating from before 1914. I saw one steamer with a clipper bow and sawn-off bowsprit, and there were still plenty of small sailing vessels in the coasting trade. The three-masted training barque, *Guanabara*, sister to the USCG *Eagle*, had come from the Germans after 1945. We never saw her under sail, and she subsequently passed to the Portuguese as the *Sagres*, replacing their old square rigger *Sagres*, which was built as the cargo-carrying windjammer *Rickmer Rickmers* in 1896, still in existence as a museum ship in Hamburg.

A cargo-carrying schooner we overtook one afternoon was making slow progress in the light airs. Her broad transom stern and 'outdoor' rudder showed no sign of propeller wash, indicating she had no auxiliary engine. Other small sailing craft abounded on the river, particularly the 'Canoas de vela' distinctive with elegant sheer, bright colours, and a sharply raking mast with a small topmast at which fluttered the Brazil ensign. Single jibs and big high-peaked gaff mainsails came in all colours, from deep russet to palest blue. Small motor-powered craft with high deck houses towed strings of native canoes, deeply laden with produce for market, including quaintly-shaped bales of rubber. Almost one thousand miles up the Amazon, off Manaos the three-masted sailing ship hulk, *Senator* lay permanently at her buoy. She was used for storing both bales of rubber and bunker coal, the latter for the aged steamers which still called occasionally.

**Brazil to New York**

New York was a first for me. From Brazil we took a large cargo of castor seed in bags and bulk,

rubber in bales, gum in cases and cartons, bales of jaborandi leaves, bags of cocoa, bags of wax, deeptanks full of castor oil (used also for aero engines), and skins of wild pig, deer, otter, alligator and jaguar in bales. Conservation was still somewhere in the future. Balsam and rosewood oil came in drums, shelled brazil nuts in cases. No. 2 hold was full of ten-ton logs from the kapok tree, with another 43 of these monsters on deck. Felled far away and floated down the river in rafts towed by small motor tugs, these logs had been in the water for months - and smelled like it! The decks and masthouses were filled with cargo as well as the holds. I remember seeing Captain Roberts and the mate poring over cargo booking lists late into the night, deciding where to stow everything. In Manaos I spent a happy Saturday afternoon persuading the dockers to stow as many bales, bags and barrels under the forecastle head as could be squeezed in. When they flagged in the equatorial heat, the third mate and I finished the task of stowing it ourselves. Satisfying work. Fully laden at nearly all times our little *Dominic* certainly paid her way on that voyage.

Sailing from Brazil in summer to New York in winter was quite a shock. But the third mate and I introduced our Brazilian lads to snow-balling, which they took up with gusto. Especially when they realised they were better shots than we were. Unloading was followed by a spell in drydock at the Bethlehem Steel yard in Brooklyn, after which we shifted round to the Booth Line regular berth, Pier 33 Brooklyn, near the Atlantic Basin, right opposite Governor's Island, Manhattan, and the Statue of Liberty.

Needless to say we all, in our various ways, had a marvellous fortnight in New York, before sailing with parts of a huge oil-refining plant on board. Much of this was loaded by the floating crane *Colossus*, though other equally heavy items were loaded by our own two jumbo derricks which had been re-rigged in the Brooklyn shipyard to accept heavier lifts. All this oil refinery cargo would be off-loaded using our own derricks at a river anchorage on the Amazon, a few miles below Manaos.

*Dominic* at New York on a much earlier occasion: shortly after she had been bought by Booth Line and renamed. *[World Ship Photo Library]*

We also loaded two cows and two bulls for Recife. They were kept in stalls on deck and looked after by the third mate. On 16th March we sailed from New York round to Norfolk, Virginia where we loaded a United Nations cargo of barrels of dried milk. When as much of this as possible had been stowed we shifted across Hampton Roads to Newport News to load 2,252 tons and 400 lbs of coal also for Recife. While we were anchored off here awaiting our loading berth a gale sprang up and we began to drag. Promptly noticed, this was stopped by steaming ahead and laying out two anchors instead of the usual one which normally held us fast in an anchorage crowded with ships. The numerous Liberties were quite outnumbered by old counter-stern vertical-straight-bar-stem tramps waiting to load for Europe which, in those stringent post-war years, was still dependent upon US coal for its power stations and domestic heating. Recife, Cabadello, Camocim anchorage, and Fortaleza came and went in steady succession as we unloaded our cargo, and resumed loading - this time for Liverpool.

Returning to the Amazon for Belem loading, instead of going alongside we anchored a mile downstream in a quiet spot sheltered by overhanging trees of the surrounding dense jungle. Leaning idly over the rail I noticed several canoes come silently under our stern, whereupon the sailors, in well drilled precision, emerged one by one from the after hatch carrying bales, boxes and bundles which were furtively lowered on lines into the canoes. Not a word was spoken. The jovial conversation and clink of glasses emanating from the Captain's cabin told me the boarding customs officers, who were on their official 'visit', were being well entertained and kept out of the way.

As soon as this little 'transfer' was completed, we weighed anchor and proceeded alongside our usual quayside berth. This (to me) unusual method of importing luxuries from New York was, it seemed, long established. Almost a way of life, which seemed to please everyone involved - including the customs.

*Dominic* loading at buoys off Manaos, one thousand miles up the Amazon on 14th May 1955. The company launch is on its way out to the vessel, which is loading Brazil nuts from the steel-hooded barge alongside. The sliding hoods were closed when the rains came, as they do very heavily up the Amazon. *[Author]*

## Home and abroad

Part of our homeward cargo was 1,200 tons of brazil nuts in bulk. Each day at sea the nuts were trimmed into furrows: one day athwartships, next day fore and aft. Six Brazilian trimmers had been signed on in Belem for this arduous work. Good surface ventilation was of the essence. The electric fans in the holds were run at maximum power, and twice daily the mate crawled round taking the cargo temperatures.

Our entry into Liverpool's King's Dock on 6th June was halted at the last minute by the dockmaster. It seemed that strikes had broken out all over the UK: railwaymen, coalminers and dockers were all out. After anchoring in the river off Cammell Laird's shipyard for 24 hours to await developments, we were diverted to Rotterdam, the next port on our itinerary. This upset some members who, we learned, had gone to great pains to stow cheaply-obtained Camel and Chesterfield cigarettes inside bags of the Rotterdam castor seed cargo. The plan had been to remove these cigarette cartons from the bags as opportunity offered in Liverpool, then sell them to known contacts. The prospect of the castor seed sacks being discharged at Rotterdam still containing the cigarettes was too hard to bear. But when we arrived alongside on that summer's evening I was amazed to see sailors emerging one by one from the castor seed hold, clothes bulging mysteriously and, with cheerful nods, walk nonchalantly past the Dutch customs officers standing by the gangway. All's well that ends well: American cigarettes were found to be in even greater demand in Holland than they would have been in Liverpool! After a call at Antwerp the British strikes ended, and we returned to Liverpool.

This had been my first visit to the continent of Europe - worldwide holiday travel had not taken off in 1955 - and it also marked the end of my first and last voyage with 'the men from Brazil'. It had been a most interesting experience, one which taught a callow young second mate how to get along with foreigners, and how the colour of your skin is unimportant. It's the man inside the skin who matters. Never again was I to be nervous in their presence, which was just as well because I subsequently sailed with Barbadian and Chinese crews in Blue Star Line. Forty years later I frequently found myself the only West European on board, my shipmates a happy mix of Indonesians and Burmese, Ghanaians, Chinese, Filipinos, Malaysians, Nigerians, and men from Montenegro.

The little *Dominic* with her British officers and Brazilian crew had taught me well. I saw her again in King's Dock, Liverpool early in 1962 and, out of sheer curiosity, went aboard. Laid up for sale, she was soon purchased by the Golden Line of Singapore, subtitled Guan Guan, owned by the Indonesian Chinese Thio family. (At the end of my seafaring career I was employed by them for nine very happy years.) At first they named her *Samodra Mas*, which is Indonesian for Golden Ocean. On 6th April 1963 she ran aground in the tricky waters off Borneo. Most of her crew left, but she was helped to refloat and assisted to Hong Kong for drydocking by a vessel of the Royal Navy. A serious accident such as stranding requires a name change in the East, and she reappeared, under the same ownership, first as *Lombardus*, then in 1965 as *Golden Ocean* (in English this time) of Hong Kong. As which I next saw and went aboard her in drydock in Singapore in 1969. Her young Chinese second mate had just joined in much the same way as I had 15 years earlier.

The end came when, on 3rd June 1971, deep laden with a cargo of magnesia clinker, she foundered after springing a leak in a storm off the Andaman Islands in the Bay of Bengal. Her people took to the boats as the ship slowly sank beneath them, and after a long row all hands were eventually rescued. As her old Chinese chief engineer subsequently reported, it had been a 'long, long low'. But, as he also remarked, 26 years was no bad age for a ship designed to participate in an assault which never took place, was it?

# THE BRITISH C1-M-AV1s

**HICKORY DALE** (above)
*Consolidated Steel Corporation Ltd., Wilmington, California, USA; 1945, 3,834gt, 339 feet overall*
*Oil engine 6-cyl. 2SCSA by the Nordberg Manufacturing Co., Milwaukee, Wisconsin, USA*
Of 239 C1-M-AV1s built, ten were transferred under bareboat charter to the British Ministry of War Transport for use in the far east. This is *Hickory Dale* on 22nd June 1946, when she was managed by the Indo China Steam Navigation Co. Ltd. The war had been over for almost a year - in fact, it was almost over when she was delivered in July 1945 - but she still carries emergency rafts. In 1947 she was returned to the United States Maritime Commission and renamed *Persian Knot* to fit in with the naming scheme adopted for most of the US-flag C1-M-AV1s (a few were given names beginning *Coastal*). It was not until 1956 that she found a commercial buyer, the Korea Shipping Corporation of Seoul, who renamed her *Kunsan*. Her career almost ended in December 1958 when she stranded at Mukho, South Korea; initial salvage attempts failed and the ship was declared a constructive total loss. However, in April 1961 her owners succeeded in refloating her, and she was repaired and renamed *Daepori* to continue in service until 1985-87.

**SHERIDAN** (below)
*Consolidated Steel Corporation Ltd., Wilmington, California, USA; 1945, 3,827gt, 339 feet overall*
*Oil engine 6-cyl. 2SCSA by General Machinery Corporation,* *Hamilton, Ohio, USA*
Of the ten C1-M-AV1s chartered to the Ministry of War Transport, just four were sold to British cargo liner companies, including *Dominic*, the subject of the previous article. The Vestey group also took *Hickory Glen*, which was allocated to Lamport and Holt Line Ltd. in 1947 as *Sheridan*. She became *Matupi* in 1960 for the Vestey-owned Austasia Line Ltd., registered in Labuan, and in 1964 was sold to Singapore owners to become *Tong Lam*. Like *Dominic*, she was to come to a sticky end. On 22nd October 1970 she ran on to Scarborough Reef in the South China Sea whilst carrying North Korean pig iron to Chittagong and broke up after being hit by a typhoon.

**BRESCIA** (above)

*Consolidated Steel Corporation Ltd., Wilmington, California, USA; 1945, 3,817gt, 339 feet overall*

*Oil engine 6-cyl. 2SCSA by the Nordberg Manufacturing Co., Milwaukee, Wisconsin, USA*

Perhaps the most surprising British owner of a utilitarian C1-M-AV1 was the then proud Cunard Line, but *Brescia* was a useful size for their Mediterranean services. She received the white waterline band which distinguished all Cunarders. Until 1947 she had been the *Hickory Isle*, and after sale in 1966 became *Timber One*, as which she returned to the Mersey at least once. In 1970, quite late in life, she was converted for a new career as a research and mining vessel, used in an attempt to lift mineral-rich nodules from the seabed. *Deepsea Miner*, as she had become, was broken up at Santander in 1974.

**HEATHMORE** (below)

*Consolidated Steel Corporation Ltd., Wilmington, California, USA; 1945, 3,825gt, 339 feet overall*

*Oil engine 6-cyl. 2SCSA by the Nordberg Manufacturing Co., Milwaukee, Wisconsin, USA*

In 1948 *Hickory Mount* became the *Heathmore* of Johnston Warren Lines Ltd., part of the Furness group, whose markings can be discerned on her diminutive funnel. Like *Brescia* she was used in Mediterranean trades. Sold in 1961, she became *Grecian Med* under the Greek flag and after 1969 the Venezuelan *Imataca*. She returned to Europe in 1972 to be broken up at Bilbao.

## METHANE PIONEER

*Walter Butler (Shipbuilders) Inc., Duluth, Minnesota, USA; 1945, 5,058gt, 339 feet overall*
*Oil engine 6-cyl. 2SCSA by the Nordberg Manufacturing Co., Milwaukee, Wisconsin, USA*

*Marline Hitch* was sold by the US Maritime Commission in 1946 and became the Panama flag *Don Aurelio* and later the Liberian *Normarti*. In 1958 she was acquired by a consortium comprising the British Gas Council and two US companies which sent her to Mobile, Alabama to be converted to a liquid natural gas carrier. Five highly-insulated tanks were fitted in her holds to carry two thousand tons of gas at -258° Fahrenheit. She was British registered as *Methane Pioneer* in the ownership of British Methane Ltd., and managed by Stephenson Clarke Ltd. After successful trials in the US she left the Gulf of Mexico in January 1959 with the first cargo of gas for Canvey Island, where it was fed into the British gas grid. A series of successful voyages established the viability of the operation, and much larger vessels were built to bring gas to the UK, although the loading point was usually Algeria and not the US. She is seen at anchor in the Thames in July 1959.

In 1967 *Methane Pioneer* was sold to Rethymnis and Kulukundis and renamed *Aristotle*, once again under the Panama flag. In 1977 she was taken in hand for a further conversion, this time at Philadelphia, and became a storage hulk for butadiene at Recife.

At least one other converted C1-M-AV1 came into the ownership of a British company, the drill ship *Dalmahoy* of Christian Salvesen Ltd.

## SOURCES AND ACKNOWLEDGEMENTS

Photographs are from the collection of John Clarkson unless otherwise credited. We thank all who gave permission for their photographs to be used, and for help in finding photographs we are particularly grateful to David Whiteside and Tony Smith of the World Ship Photo Library; to Ian Farquhar, Bill Laxon, Peter Newall, Ivor Rooke, William Schell, George Scott; to David Hodge and Bob Todd of the National Maritime Museum; Dr. David Jenkins of the Welsh Industrial and Maritime Museum; and the other museums and institutions listed.

Research sources have included the *Registers* of William Schell and Tony Starke, *Lloyd's Register, Lloyd's Confidential Index, Lloyd's War Losses, Mercantile Navy Lists*, and *Marine News*. Use of the facilities of the World Ship Society's Central Record, the Guildhall Library, the Public Record Office and Lloyd's Register of Shipping are gratefully acknowledged. Particular thanks also to William Schell and John Bartlett for information, to Heather Fenton for editorial and indexing work, and to Marion Clarkson for accountancy services.

### Bibby four masted ships
Books consulted were E.W. Paget-Tomlinson, *The Bibby Line: 175 years of achievement*, Bibby Line Ltd., Liverpool, 1982; Nigel Watson *The Bibby Line: 1807-1990*, James and James, London, 1990; Duncan Hawes, *The Burma Boats*, TCL Publications, Uckfield, 1996; Arnold Kludas, *Great Passenger Ships of the World*, PSL, Cambridge,1976; C.R. Vernon-Gibbs, *Great Passenger Liners of the Five Oceans*, 1963; Lawrence Dunn, *Famous Liners of the Past - Belfast built*, Sea Breezes, Liverpool, 1963; John Kennedy, *The History of Steam Navigation*, Charles Birchall, Liverpool, 1903; J.H. Isherwood *Steamers of the Past*, Sea Breezes, Liverpool, 1996; M. Moss and J.R. Hume, *Shipbuilders to the World*, Blackstaff, Belfast,1986; H.T. Lenton and J.J. Colledge *Warships of the World. Part 4: Auxiliary Fighting Vessels*, Ian Allan, London, 1962. In addition, information has come from *Sea Breezes; Ships Monthly; Marine News; Directory of Shipowners, Shipbuilders & Marine Engineers for 1915, 1930, 1939, 1949, and 1958*; the Guildhall Library, and the library of Lloyd's Register.

### Whitbury Shipping Co. Ltd.
Thanks are due to a number of people but in particular to Trevor Jewsbury and Jack Whiting who shared their experiences with the author. Thanks also to the staff at Lloyds Register of Shipping and the Guildhall Library for their assistance in writing the article.

### Torquay Harbour in the 1930s
Thanks are due to Wilfred Hore for allowing the use of his paper for the University College of the South West of England, *A Detailed Account of Trade of Torquay Harbour 1924-1935*, a copy of which is lodged in Torquay Library, to whom thanks are also due for the use of their facilities, including *Lloyd's Registers* borrowed from Exeter Library. Thanks are also due to Roy Fenton and the resources of the World Ship Society's Central Record for many of the ship histories; to John Pike, former chief librarian of Torbay and now a writer and local historian, not only for his books listed below but also for guidance in the early stages; to Torquay Museum for the use of their photographs; and to David Clement of the South West Maritime History Society for help with the identification of early sailing ships in Torquay harbour; and to L. Mee for help with typing. Sources used include: *Tall Ships in Torbay and Torquay: The Place and People, A Centenary History*, both by John Pike; *No Gallant Ship* by Michael Bouquet; *A History of Torquay*, by Percy Russell; *The New Maritime History of Devon, Volume 2*, especially the papers by David J Starkey, Robin Craig and John Travis; *Pleasure Steamers*, by Bernard Cox; *Everard of Greenhithe*, by K. S. Garrett, and *Carebeka 1939-1983* by J.H.Anderiesse, E.A. Kruidhof and J. Oostmeijer, both published by the World Ship Society; *Coast Lines* by Norman L. Middlemiss; *The Coastwise Trade*, by George Thompson; *Lost Ships of the West Country*, by Martin Langley and Edwina Small; *Coasting Sailorman* by Capt. 'Harry' Bagshaw, Albert Bagshaw and Richard Walsh; *River Medway and the Swale*, by Robert Simper; *Ships and Ship Models*, May 1933, published by Percival Marshall; and *British Nationalised Shipping* by W. Paul Clegg and John S. Styring.

### POLSKAROB
The major source for the history of ROBUR was *Ksiega Statków Polskich 1918-1945*, volume 2, by Jerzy Miciński, Bohdan Huras and Marek Twardowski, Gdansk 1996. Also consulted was *Flota Spod Bialo-Czerwonez*, by Jan Piwowonski, Nasza Ksiegarnia, 1989. The fleet list was compiled by Jerzy Swieszkowski and Roy Fenton, with help from Bill Schell and Bohdan Huras.

# PUTTING BURNS AND LAIRD STRAIGHT

The Ships in Focus policy is to strive hard to get the facts in our publications right, to encourage our contributors to do likewise, and to print corrections if we err. We are pleased to report that the comments received so far on our latest pictorial history, *Ships in Focus Burns and Laird*, include only minor corrections to the histories of the ships represented. However, they do suggest that we were misled as to what is shown in two photographs which were included.

Taking the textual corrections first, the German submarine which sank the *Fern* (page 24) was U 104 not U 194. On page 32, the names of the hull and engine builders of *Duke of Argyll* were transposed. John Russell points out that the *Maple* was built by Ailsa's Ayr yard rather than at Troon (page 41).

## The fourth ship on the slip

The rear endpaper showed the motorships *Lairdscrest*, *Lairdswood*, and *Lairdsbank* being built at Harland and Wolff's Queen's Island yard on 26th June 1936. Based on information on the back of the print, we reported that the fourth vessel on the building berth was Bank Line's *Ernebank*. We should have looked closer, as the newbuilding has only three hatches, and is too small for *Ernebank*. George Gardner was the first to spot this, and suggests that the vessel is actually Union-Castle's *Walmer Castle* (906/1936). This is confirmed by an entry which Colin Campbell turned up in *Shipbuilding and Shipping Record* for 30th July 1936, which has a view of the four vessels from the opposite direction, noting that the fourth is a 'small coaster building for the Union-Castle Mail Steamship Co. Ltd.'

Reference to Peter Newall's excellent *Union-Castle Line: a Fleet History* indicates that *Walmer Castle* was built as a feeder ship to run between Southampton, Hamburg and Bremen. She was launched on 17th September 1936, exactly two weeks after the *Lairdsbank*. She bears a strong resemblance to the three Burns and Laird vessels, having slightly heavier cargo gear and an extended superstructure. Unlike the Burns and Laird sisters, however, she had only a single screw.

The little motorship's life was tragically short, ending only days after she set out in the outbound Gibraltar convoy OG 74, the first for which she was to act as a rescue ship. On 21st September 1941, whilst catching up with the convoy after rescuing survivors from *Empire Moat* (2,922/1941) and *Baltallinn* (1,303/1920), the *Walmer Castle* was bombed by a German Focke-Wulff Fw200 and set on fire, subsequently being sunk by an escort vessel. As well as her own complement, she had on board over 80 survivors of ships previously sunk, and casualties in her sinking totalled 31.

## Not the Dublin Custom House

On page 10 we reproduced an old postcard which we believed to show the *Rose* of 1867 off the Custom House at Dublin. David Hodge and Bob Todd of the National Maritime Museum and Ian Wilson have pointed out that it is not the Dublin Custom House, and this is confirmed by reference to page 67 of *Record* 6, which shows a Guinness boat alongside the real one. Looking at the lighter moored by the stern of the *Rose*, Ian hazards a guess that it may be on the Thames, and photographs in the NMM

*Walmer Castle [F.W. Hawks]*

certainly confirm this. This raises the question of what was the Glasgow-based *Rose* doing in the Thames, and Ian Wilson suggests that this is not, in fact, the right ship, pointing out that the vessel in the photograph is too short for the 180-foot *Rose*, and - with her flush deck - that she does not appear to have been built for the rigours of the waters off the north of Ireland. Interestingly, the funnel colours of the ship in the photograph correspond with at least one of the colour schemes used by Laird. His previous *Rose* was a paddler, and the 1871 *Mercantile Navy List* does not list any other steamer of the name which would fit. Suggestions are welcome.

## The Clyde to Heligoland

Readers have been generous with comments which add to the information in *Burns and Laird*. James Cooper follows up the entry on page 16 concerning the paddle steamer *Cobra*, which was sold by Burns to Ballin's Dampfschiffs Rhederei Gesellschaft of Hamburg. This was Albert Ballin's own company, his 'hobby' line as opposed to his HAPAG business. *Cobra* was used on a summer service between Hamburg and Heligoland and the North Friesian islands. In 1897 owners became Nordsee Linie DG. In 1902 *Cobra* was chartered by HAPAG for the winter season sailings between Genoa and Nice via San Remo and Monte Carlo. At the end of this season she returned to Hamburg for Heligoland sailings, and continued alternating on these routes until 1906. Meanwhile, HAPAG had purchased the Nordsee Linie DG in January 1905. Painted white, *Cobra* continued in their service in the summer months until the First World War, although there was a break in the French Riviera sailings between 1909 and 1911. Although intended to go to France as reparations at the end of the war, she remained with HAPAG and was sold in December 1921 to Mahr und Beyer for breaking up at Wismar.

## Funnels and masts

Charles Waine comments on the funnel colours of the *Adder* on page 16, and suggests that they are buff as expected and not red, as they appear darker than the red ensign. He points out that early photographic film was not particularly sensitive to red, so that it appears almost black. This explains why *Lairdsrose* appears to have a plain black funnel in the upper photograph on page 38. The suggestion in the captions to *Spaniel* on page 20 that the fidded masts may have been to reduce height for passage of the newly-opened Manchester Ship Canal is challenged by Charles Waine. Plans of the slightly larger *Magpie* and *Vulture*, which also have fidded masts, show their masts are 75 feet high, only one foot less than the maximum allowed on the Ship Canal. He doubts that a regular trader would go to the trouble of unshipping topmasts and still having very limited clearance. The *Setter* - which was built for running up the Canal - has masts just 35 feet high. Charles suggests that the masts were fidded to facilitate construction, with steel lower masts and wooden topmasts.

## Could it be the *Titanic* ?

The editors have felt there is very little left to say about the *Titanic*, but it has been pointed out that the unfinished ship which the *Viper* is passing in the photograph on page 28 could well be the celebrated White Star liner herself. Visible features, such as windows, ports, deck and the foremast, match those of the *Titanic*, although a foreshortening effect in the photograph makes the ship look unduly short. It would be interesting to know if this photograph has appeared in any of the myriad of books on the *Titanic*, it being too much to hope that this is a first for *Record*!

## *Penguin*

Bill Laxon comments on the photograph of *Penguin* on page 8. It shows her stranded in the old entrance to Nelson, probably on 16th November 1895 - she stranded there on four or five occasions. Bill has kindly supplied the excellent view of her seen opposite, taken at Nelson soon after arrival in New Zealand and with yards on the foremast - this would have been more how she looked in Burns' days.

*Cobra* in German service, probably running to Heligoland. *[James Cooper collection]*

"AGAINST the TIDE".
TYREE, 1026.

# PUTTING THE RECORD STRAIGHT

Letters, additions, amendments and photographs relating to articles in any issues of *Record* are welcomed. Letters may be lightly edited.

## RAKAIA sails home

I came across Ships in Focus *New Zealand and Federal Lines* and read it with great interest, particularly the write-up on the *Rakaia*. I was an engineer on my second trip when the engine breakdown occurred just out of New York.

The engine was an eight-cylinder Burmeister & Wain double-acting, two-stroke, and the number eight piston rod snapped off at the cross-head. The con-rod came through the side of the engine, and a crankcase explosion occurred at the same time. Luckily no-one was in the vicinity at the time and no-one was hurt. I recollect it was on the midnight-to-four watch. We stripped the unit right out and after about three days we managed to get the engine going again on seven cylinders. The normal engine revs were about 104rpm, but because the engine was now completely out of balance and crankshaft had twisted about two degrees, we were able to get it going at 18 to 20rpm. The cadets on *Rakaia* were put to work making up and rigging the sails, and with both sails and engine we eventually arrived in Liverpool at the top speed of about 4 knots.

As your book suggests there was a tremendous spirit between officers and crew - even the old man himself, Captain Lawsen, was helping out in the engine room. I think the chief engineer, McNair, was on his last trip prior to retirement.

A Watts, Watts ship circled around us offering assistance, so the Captain had the crew prepared to repel boarders if necessary. We were also short of certain foods and water, so the Captain decreed that only the engine room staff could have showers and bacon and eggs.
COLIN J FRANCIS, 8 Manse Place, Redwood, Christchurch 8005, New Zealand.

## Studying biology and psychology on *Rose Hilda*

As 'a rather elderly gentleman' of 72 it was a delight to read Stephen Daniels' piece on steam drifters (*Record* 12) which included the drifter/trawler, *Rose Hilda*. It stimulated memories of over 50 years' ago when I joined her at Fleetwood as a college lecturer hoping to investigate some biological aspects of trawling. Instead, it turned out as an investigation into human psychology.

At the time she was fitted out as a trawler and owned by W.J.E. Green of Winterton. Her skipper, Ted King, had a crew of mate, two leading hands, two deckhands, the engineer or 'driver', fireman, bunker boy, and cook. The skipper of her a sister ship, the *Romany Rose*, was Walter Rudd, from Winterton and a former Prunier Trophy winner: I can still recall his rendering of *'I've been a wild rover ...'*

*Rose Hilda* worked around the UK coast, whilst *Romany Rose* worked out of Yarmouth as a drifter: this made the former more of a romany than the latter!

My arrival was greeted with total disinterest other than a thumb indicating an empty bunk which was mine. My tour of the ship showed a bridge with its wood-grain effect of brown paint, and inside very sparse. The technology consisted of the radio direction finder and also a radio - vital for inter-ship conversations, and for the BBC programme *Listen with Mother*. The engine room was half flooded with water: reporting this I gathered it would be dealt with, and was advised to leave the running of the ship to those who knew. The hull was battered from numerous collisions occurring on leaving and berthing - something I saw personally later.

It was midsummer and the crew were enjoying their shore leave of a few days spent mainly in Blackpool. Having turned in, my attempts at sleep were periodically disturbed by the noisy arrival of my crewmates eager to have a look at the green hand. Towards early morning a very corpulent person slid down the vertical accommodation ladder, gathered himself up, and went head first into what looked like a wardrobe - the skipper's cabin.

After obtaining the vital shoreside refreshment the majority of the crew returned for our departure at high water the next day, and went to their berths whilst the 'teetotallers' took the ship out.

The trip occupied 14 days of monotonous and continual shooting and hauling, each trawl lasting around three hours and followed by the sorting, gutting, and packing away of the catch in the ice of the fishroom, a place I often sought for its coolness and for some peace from the continuous deck noise and four-letter word repetition used somewhat as a form of therapy in the harsh environment.

I found in everyone aboard a total honesty and sincerity, and often found myself the recipient of their confidences. I would be sharply told to shut up if I was whistling, or talking about farmers whom they heartily detested.

We fished around the Chickens and the Kish, and this produced fine hauls of hake, skate or roker, conger eels which lay alive around the deck for days, and much 'gash' from the sea bed. On one occasion Ted King pointed out some Welsh skippers from Milford Haven or Conwy speaking in the vernacular on the radio, and I then acted as his informer and translator against my fellow countrymen.

The cook, Ernie, produced delightful, well-cooked meals, inevitably including dumplings (which I called dough balls thereby causing offence). The freshly cooked selection of fish, straight off the deck was eaten by picking what we fancied from a large pan. Dispensing with cutlery we used our fingers, licking off the delicious tender sweet flesh. Ernie's freshly cooked bread was unbeatable, and the raising of the dough took place between his bunk blankets which he had warmed during his siesta.

The engine room with its triple expansion steam engine was a joy to watch and listen to, but I would evacuate the place when Milky, the engineer, opened and recharged the acetylene gas generator. Sadly I incurred his annoyance when, without permission, I took pages from his old copy of *The News of the World* for the purpose of hygiene in the convenience consisting of an open-ended oil drum and a bucket on a lanyard.

I remember being sharply reprimanded by the mate when tucking into my first meal aboard: the skipper ate first. This came as something of a shock in such a tough environment. Later, as we sat around the table, there was a mighty banging and roaring from beneath and all hands disappeared into their surrounding bunks to escape

*Rose Hilda* sailing from Fleetwood, probably in the 1920s.

Leading hands aboard *Rose Hilda* (above) and her foredeck with removable gallows and the cran pole (below). *[Fred Kilgour]*

*Girl Eileen*, probably at Wick. *[James Pottinger]*

warping drum on one side, and horizontal shaft extension to take a handle for manual operation on the other side.

JAMES A. POTTINGER, 1 Jesmond Circle, Bridge of Don, Aberdeen AB22 8WX. email: japwait@waitrose.com

harm. It transpired that the connecting bolts had broken away from the connecting rod and the main bearing. The 'driver', seemingly unaffected, was smiling up at several faces peering down into his domain. Later I was to help him retrieve the banana-shaped bolts from the most evil-smelling bilge water one could encounter.

Shortage of tobacco, sleep, temper, and conversation all set in towards the end of the trip. For me it was a very close encounter with the differing personalities of a group of men working in a very close environment and under great mental and physical stress.

I treasure these memories which remain so clear and am proud to have shared this voyage with such fine fellows from Winterton.

FRED KILGOUR, Y Gorlan, 21 Meiriadog Road, Colwyn Bay, Conwy LL29 9NR.

## Stern matters

I would like to add to the steam drifters' article (*Record* 12, page 238) which mentions preferences for types of stern. The tug-type stern was favoured on wooden boats as being much less susceptible to damage when in a crowded dock or harbour. The heavy rubbing strake at deck level offered greater protection than would be afforded by the wooden top rail of the bulwarks on an overhanging counter stern. Few wooden drifters were built with a counter stern, but one such was the *Girl Eileen*, YH 766, built by Fellows and Co. of Yarmouth in 1910 (see photo).

A possible reason for the extra length of the *A. Rose* is that she was designed to box her catch at sea. And one correction: *Fortitude* has a cruiser stern, not a counter stern as stated in the caption on page 239.

I wonder if any other reader has noted the unusual steam capstan on the stern of the *Ben Seyr* (page 225)? It would appear to be of the Beccles-type seen on herring motor and steam drifters: there is a steel box over the pistons and gearing on top, the same long whelps, small

## Firing on too many cylinders

*Swans on the Lakes*, the nostalgic look (*Record* 12) at the ships built at Wallsend earlier this century for the Great Lakes is full of interest for me but, without wishing to be critical, I would like to point out three instances in which the shorthand used by *Lloyd's Register* in pre-war days has apparently misled the caption writer in his description of the ships' machinery.

In the case of twin screw ships, *Lloyd's Register* gave the total number of engine cylinders. Thus, the *Toiler* was fitted with two four-cylinder diesel engines, each of 180 BHP, not with eight-cylinder engines. Similarly, the *Tynemount* entry is confusing because she had two six-cylinder Mirrlees diesels, each driving an electric generator. The output of these two generators fed into a 500 HP electric motor, which was coupled directly to the single propeller shaft. Finally, the ill-fated *Joseph Medill* had two five-cylinder MAN diesel engines, each of 500 BHP, and each engine drove its own propeller.

When it comes to the machinery, I am surprised how some very knowledgeable ship researchers fail to appreciate what the *Register* is telling them. Another common pitfall is the quoting of nominal horse power (NHP) when the actual machinery horsepower is not available. NHP is really quite meaningless, being derived from a Lloyd's formula and intended as a basis for calculating machinery survey fees. As a rough guide NHP usually works out as about one-fifth of the actual horse power, but this is very approximate.

JOHN B. HILL, The Hollies, Wall, Hexham, Northumberland NE46 4EQ.

## It takes one to correct one

During the Second World War the submarine depot stationed in Rothesay Bay was HMS *Cyclops*, 'mother' to the 7th Submarine Flotilla. HMS *Montclare*, quoted in error in my article *It takes one to know one* (*Record* 11, page 173), did not take over the prominent location until 1947, when she became base for the 3rd Submarine Flotilla. She was built in 1921 as the Canadian Pacific liner of the same name and spent her war years as an armed merchant cruiser, and then as a destroyer depot ship.

IAN W. MUIR, 10 Sir Gabriel Wood Court, 221 Finnart Street, Greenock, PA16 8JD.

## Off and on the Canal

Many thanks for the *Ellesmere Port Quartet* article in *Record* 12 which was of great interest to me - it was whilst walking along the quayside of Douglas Inner Harbour in 1962 watching the Ramsey coasters unloading coal that I first became interested in ships. This interest grew and still continues.

I would point out a minor matter relating to one of the accompanying photographs. The caption to the picture on page 219 states that it shows a ship in the pontoon at Ellesmere Port. The presence of the quay with a railway line in the foreground, however, suggests to me that the pontoon shown is the one at the Dry Docks Co.'s Mode Wheel yard, with Salford Quay in the foreground. The Mode Wheel pontoon was moored alongside the yard just downstream of the dry dock entrances, more or less in the Mode Wheel Locks sluiceway. I believe it was brought into use in September 1894. I am not sure exactly when it was removed or scrapped but would guess that it went in the mid 1960s.

On an entirely different matter, I would like to mention a point of interest to me in relation to *Record* 11 - the feature on Ken Cunnington and his picture, reproduced on page 161, of the tug *Rixton* assisting the Norwegian tanker *Amica*. Another of Mr. Cunnington's pictures featuring the *Amica* appeared in the very first edition of Ian Allan's *Ocean Ships* in the early 1960s. This also showed the *Amica* in the Canal with topmasts hinged forward for upper Canal passage but the accompanying fleet list gave its measurements as being 10,191 gross tons with length 542 feet and beam 64 feet. I had often puzzled about this ship navigating the Ship Canal as with those measurements it would have been very marginal. Now, however, the riddle is solved as you have shown the tonnage as 5,010 and that the ship in the *Ocean Ships* photograph was a different *Amica* to the one shown in the fleet list. However, a further interesting point arises as the *Ocean Ships* picture shows the ship with a much shorter funnel than the one with which she is endowed in the *Record* photo and this was not shortened for Ship Canal passage. Perhaps the ship was re-engined as a motor ship at some stage.

Thanks once again for an excellent publication.
KEN LOWE, 15 Oaks Close, Horsham, West Sussex RH12 4TZ

*Ken is quite correct: C.H. Sörensen's* Amica *of 1946 was originally fitted with a compound four-cylinder steam engine made by her builders, Fredrikstads MV A/S, but this was replaced with a US-built oil engine in 1953. The photograph of* Amica *in* Record *11 showing her with a tall funnel producing much smoke was clearly taken before 1953. Ed.*

### Lucerne elucidated

The photo caption says that identification of the *Lucerne* is problematic (*Record* 12, page 219). Perhaps we can help with this. The ship was built by Laird Brothers at Birkenhead for J. and A. Allan of Glasgow. She was launched in March 1878 and on 27th September 1879 sailed on her maiden voyage from Glasgow for South America. According to Duncan Haws' *Merchant Fleets in Profile 3* she was sold in 1898 to the United States Government for use as a transport, but this is incorrect. In *North Atlantic Seaway* N.R.P. Bonsor says 'reported sold to US Government.' In fact, she was sold to A. Harvey and Co., St. John's, Newfoundland. This agrees with the entry in *Lloyd's Register* for 1899-1900. The *Lucerne* was wrecked in Trinity Bay, Newfoundland on 3rd February 1901 when on a voyage from Ardrossan to St John's, Newfoundland with coal, with the loss of all hands. The wreckage was badly charred, indicating that the ship was on fire at the time of her loss.

David Hodge has checked the movements of the *Lucerne* for the period 1893 to 1901 and found that she visited Manchester on three occasions. In 1898 she passed Eastham inward bound on 4th July and passed out of Eastham locks on 12th July. In 1899 she was in Manchester from 15th to 23rd June, and whilst in the Eastham Channel she had a minor collision with the steamer *Comorin* (563/1863), which resulted in slight damage which might have required attention by Manchester Dry Docks. *Lucerne's* third arrival was on 26th December 1899, sailing on 9th January 1900.

Perhaps someone can say if any of Stott's vessels were in port on any of these three occasions.
BOB G. TODD, National Maritime Museum, Greenwich, London SE10 9NF.

*Bob and David's painstaking research on* Lucerne's *visits to Manchester certainly support Ken Lowe's suggestion in the previous letter that the photograph with the* Lucerne *in the foreground on page 219 shows the Manchester pontoon, and not that at Ellesmere Port. Ed.*

### Orara error

In *Record* 11 on page 182, you have described the wrong *Orara* in the caption. The 1894 *Orara* of 66 tons and 71 feet long was built at Blackwall by R. Davis and owned by D. Henderson as you say, but was wrecked at Wooloolga, New South Wales, on 30th December 1895 after her shaft broke and she drifted on to a reef. The vessel in the photo is the 298 gross tons, 133.8 feet long *Orara* built in 1898 by H. Hardman at Jervis Bay and owned by G.W. Nicoll of Sydney. She was the vessel wrecked at Tweed Heads on 16th February 1899, as you say.
BILL LAXON, Waimarana, Upper Whangateau Road, PO Box 171, Matakana 1240, New Zealand.

### British Industry failing

With reference to the exhibition ship, *British Exhibitor* (*Record* 12, page 201), it may be of interest to your readers that this was not the first such venture to fail. In the early 1920s, when shipbuilding was going through one of its periodic slumps, Swan, Hunter and Wigham Richardson suffered two cancelled orders in quick succession, making their survival that much harder. The first was for the lead ship of the 48,000-ton 'I' class battle cruiser, which fell foul of the Washington Naval Treaty which limited capital ship construction. The second was for a 20,000-ton triple-screw motor ship for British Trade Ship Ltd., London, to be powered by Neptune diesels and named *British Industry*. The plans for this ship are held in the National Maritime Museum, and the yard number indicates that it would have been built at Wallsend.
IAN RAE, 196 Broadway, Tynemouth, Tyne and Wear NE30 3RY.

### Bits on Bazeleys

I have a completion and a substantial addition to two entries in Bazeleys fleet list (*Record* 12).

8. *Gervase*

As *Leonardo* she was abandoned after striking a wreck on 23rd December 1929 in position 42.17 north, 05.36 east, whilst on a voyage from Baia to Malaga with clay.

16. *Solway*

As *Meigle* she was refitted 1942 and returned to service (name unchanged) owned by Shaw S.S. Co. (Newfoundland) Ltd. (G. T. Shaw, manager), St. John's, Newfoundland. She was wrecked 19th July 1947 at Marine Cove, one mile north of St. Shotts, St. Mary's Bay, Newfoundland whilst on a voyage from Charlottetown, Prince Edward Island, to St. John's, Newfoundland with general cargo and livestock.
BILL SCHELL, 334 South Franklin Street, Holbrook MA 02343, USA.

*Snowdrop*

## *Snowdrop* on Whit Tuesday

The photograph of the Mersey ferry, *Snowdrop* (*Record* 5, page 62) recalled happy childhood memories.

I was born in Runcorn, and after the traditional Whit Monday walks, we youngsters greatly looked forward to the following day, Whit Tuesday. On this day we boarded the *Snowdrop* which departed from Runcorn Wall at 8.00 am, and called at Weston Point to embark more passengers plus the Weston Silver Prize band. At 08.30 am we departed Weston Point, sailing down the Canal to Liverpool, and thence on to the delights of New Brighton. After a smashing day (the weather was always good!), the return trip departed from New Brighton at 7.00 pm arriving back at Runcorn Wall at 9.45 pm. All this heaven cost one shilling for children and was organised by Weston Methodist Church, the period being the late 1920s to early 1930s. Are there any other *Record* readers who remember these trips?

Captain N.E. BANNER, 90 Tarbet Drive, Bolton BL2 6LX.

## D for disaster

*Record* 12 is a delight, as usual, though I thought it remarkable that Rowan Hackman did not see fit to mention the outstanding event in the career of the *Darro*, if not of the whole D class: the ramming and sinking, on 21st February 1917, of Elder Dempster's *Mendi* (4,230/1905) in dense fog some 12 miles off the Isle of Wight, with the loss of 656 lives (mostly members of a South African Native Labour Corps battalion on their way to the French theatre of conflict), surely one of the worst maritime accidents of the twentieth century not directly attributable to warfare. Facts, naturally, from Cowden and O'Duffy's *The Elder Dempster Fleet History 1852-1985*.

CHRISTY MAC HALE, 142 Moscow Drive, Liverpool L13 7DL

## Maritime Menageries

The Messageries Maritimes article brought back a flood of memories. When we passed one of their magnificent ships at sea or saw one in port, our first trippers were, of course, told that this was a French company whose name translated into English as Maritime Menageries. The world's oldest company - our lads where told - their first ship being Captain Noah's *Ark* ...

My first close-to memory of MM came in December 1961 in Hamburg where I was attending the installation of the *South Africa Star's* 180-ton derrick at the Howaldswerke shipyard. A gloomy, foggy afternoon. Looking up I was astonished to see the name *Laos*, followed by a row of dark portholes and windows sliding silently past, the white-painted ship only just becoming visible in the gloom, 20 feet away.

Two years later the *South Africa Star* was in Sydney when I became friendly with the captain of the *Polynésie* and his ship. Lying at Circular Quay with the magnificent backdrop of The Bridge she was indeed yacht-like - painted white, including the funnel. My last encounter with them was in 1968 when, for my sins, I joined that happy international band of brothers incarcerated on the Great Bitter Lake in the Suez Canal as a result of the 1967 Six Days' War. For four months I was mate of the *Scottish Star*, joining and leaving her via Cairo airport. There were 13 other trapped ships - three more British, two Swedish, two Polish, two West German, an American, a Czechoslovakian, a Bulgarian, and one other.

This was the French member of the Great Bitter Lakes Association (GBLA), as we called ourselves, the *Sindh*. She was not one of the passenger ships mentioned in Peter Newall's splendid article, but a cargo ship whose funnel the company had never got round to embellishing with their houseflag and therefore remained plain shiny black. With not much to do on the Lake we made our own entertainment: monthly sailing boat regattas, weekly five-a-side deck football, table tennis ... We even staged our own GBLA Olympic Games in which yours truly won a bronze medal for rowing. (Still got it: my boat came third out of three.) But the only chap to have his wife aboard was the French captain, and to our salt-and-sand-rimmed eyes the sight of this delightful sun-tanned brunette in her yellow bikini whizzing past water-skiing was indeed a tonic. They were never short of invitations to dinner, though I suppose it went without saying that the *Sindh's* Senegal chef provided the best cooking on the Lake - real French cuisine. He even made delectable delicacies out of our weevil-ridden raisin cargo.

Captain A.W. KINGHORN, 15 Kendal Avenue, Cullercoats, North Shields, Tyne and Wear NE30 3AQ

## Canadian ships, British numbers

I found the article on the Canadian-built ships for the Shipping Controller in *Record* 11 most interesting, but would like to add the following.

The Shipping Controller ordered 42 steel ships and requisitioned six more already building in Canada. He also ordered 46 wooden-hulled steamers. The authority for this is a summary and list of orders (in the UK, USA, Canada, Japan, and China) and purchases prepared by the Shipping Controller dated May 1918 now in the Public Record Office, Kew (MT25/56/30616). Len Sawyer did not have access to this when he compiled *Standard Ships of World War 1*.

*War Halifax* is shown as Southern Salvage Co. yard number 5; and *War Wasp* and *War Bee* were Nova Scotia and Coal Co. numbers 2 and 3 respectively. The yard numbers shown in the summary of the wooden ships differ from those in Len's book in 21 cases, and there are three additions.

The Shipping Controller gives intended names for several steel ships from the Polson Ironworks as *War Scorpio*, *War Aquila*, *War Hermes*, and *War Pegasus*. I believe these correspond to yard numbers 147 to 150 in Len's book.

DAVID BURRELL, 63 Avisyard Avenue, Cumnock, Ayrshire KA18 3BJ.

## Slapped wrists

The author of *Ellesmere Port Quartet* was mortified to realise that he had put a photograph of the wrong *Ben Varrey* in his article on page 223 of *Record* 12. No amount of pleading about being rushed can excuse him, as the superstructure of the *Ben Varrey* shown, the first of the name, is totally different from that of the Ellesmere Port-built vessel, whilst the second *Ben Varrey* could never have been in Preston under this name together with *Penstone*. *Ben Varrey* (1) was built in 1914 at Alloa as *Whitestone*, being bought by Ramsey Steamship Co. Ltd. in 1917 and renamed two years later. She lasted in the fleet until 1946, and after a couple of months as *Gloucesterbrook*, was sold to Danish owners who put a diesel into her, and continued trading her until 1977. As an act of contrition, the accompanying photograph of the real *Ben Varrey* (2) is included. It was taken by George Osbon on 9th June 1957, almost three months after she arrived at Dublin to be broken up by Hammond Lane Foundry Ltd. Although her wheelhouse and funnel have gone, the quayside is remarkably free of scrap, and it must be assumed that she had been temporarily moved from the breakers' wharf. *[World Ship Photo Library, Osbon collection no 2914]*

Whilst wrists are being slapped, the editor holds out his other one for a statement in the captions to Ken Cunnington's photographs on page 162 of *Record* 11 that T. and J. Harrison had four Liberties. As both Alan Phipps and D.G. Barton have pointed out, they had a total of ten: *Colonial* (later *Planter*), *Historian*, *Scholar*, *Sculptor*, *Senator*, *Speaker*, *Specialist*, *Statesman*, *Student*, and *Successor*.

*As a footnote to the story of the Cammell Laird-built* La Playa *of 1923, which was pieced together in* Records *5 (pages 24-25), 6 (pages 113-114), and 7 (page 186) Soren Thorsoe has supplied this excellent shot of the diesel-electric fruiter laid up as* Arab World *off Ambelaika in 1965. She had been bought by John S. Latsis in 1964, and it seems quite possible that she did not trade under his ownership, as she was broken up at La Spezia in 1968, although Soren reports that she was not present off Ambelaika when he visited in 1967. The name* Arab World *was probably chosen by Latsis to curry favour with the Saudis; as Anthony Cooke relates on page 155 of* Record *11, in 1963 he put a couple of large liners into the pilgrim trade for this reason.*

# SHIPS IN FOCUS

## Publications

## 18, Franklands, Longton, Preston, PR4 5PD

## QUALITY BOOKS FROM CLARKSONS - LIST B14

John & Marion Clarkson concentrate on books from **Ships in Focus** along with books of a similar high quality from other 'top of the range' publishers. We try to list only books that we would be happy to have in our own library and which conform to our own high production standards both in the reproduction of photographs and informative text. Our delivery charges are economical, all consignments are extremely well packed and we give a prompt service.

Payment may be made by including your remittance with your order. If you wish you may pay by Mastercard, Visa or VisaDelta, adding the appropriate details to the order form. You may also order by phone using our credit card order line 01772 612855. **POST AND PACKING ARE NOT INCLUDED IN THE PRICES SHOWN.**

We now have our own website with a complete listing of available books which will be updated monthly. In the next month or two a listing of photographs will be added to the website. The address of our website is;- www.shipsinfocus.co.uk and our e-mail address for orders sales@shipsinfocus.co.uk

*An important new publication – available in November*

## British Shipping Fleets

*British Shipping Fleets* contains detailed histories and fully-illustrated fleet lists of six interesting and significant shipping companies:

| | |
|---|---|
| **Manchester Liners** | **Fishers of Newry** |
| **J.T.Rennie** | **The Carron Company** |
| **Cardiff Hall Line** | **Runciman (London) Ltd.** |

*British Shipping Fleets* has been written by a team of experienced and well-known maritime historians – David Burrell, Roy Fenton, Peter Newall, Sean Patterson and Graeme Somner – to provide definitive histories of significant shipping companies too small for a book of their own. An A4-sized, 192-page hardback, it is compiled to the same exacting standards as *Record* and includes photographs of every ship possible. With a mix of liner and tramp, ocean and coastal companies, *British Shipping Fleets* offers a broad look at the subject which everyone interested in shipping history should have.

Published by Ships in Focus, *British Shipping Fleets* is available at £24.00 plus postage

**SHIPS IN FOCUS RECORD 13** Bibby's Four masters (2), Whitbury Shipping, Two funnel tankers, Torquay Harbour in 1930's, Polskarob –Polish Colliers, Port Line's Golden Era, DOMINIC and her Brazilian Crew, British C1-M-AV1s, Putting Burns & Laird Straight, *S/b £7.00*

## NEW PUBLICATIONS (or new to our list)

**FURNESS WITHY VOLUME 2** – by Duncan Haws, includes Manchester Liners, Houlders, Alexander, Prince and Rio Cape Lines. His largest book to date covering 632 ships. S/b £21.00

**CORY TOWAGE LTD., a Group history** by W Harvey The latest WSS publication due out later this month, 224 pages including 8 pages plus endpapers in colour and over 300 photographs. A4, *H/b £30.00*

**FIFTY DYNAMIC YEARS – WSS commemoration of the Millennium** – Coasters, Aircraft Carriers, Flags & Funnels, Bulkers & Tankers, Blue Funnel and Liner Development, A5 72 pages *S/b £6.00*

**SCHIFFAHRT IM BILD/SHIPPING IN PICTURES - CONTAINER SHIPS (1)** The photographs are excellent and although text is in German one can work out basic details of each ship's career. (now in stock) *H/b £14.50*

**SCHIFFAHRT IM BILD/SHIPPING IN PICTURES - MOTOR COASTERS (1)** *H/b £14.50*
**(more books in this series are planned)**

**SCHIFFAHRT IM BILD/SHIPPING IN PICTURES – CARGO LINERS (II)** (due October) *H/b £14.50*

**SCHEEPVAART 2000 by** G J de Boer. The 24th edition of this well-known yearbook of Benelux shipping. In Dutch but always worth having. *S/b £17.00*

**IMAGES OF ENGLAND / LIVERPOOL DOCKS,** compiled by Michael Stammers of Liverpool Maritime Museum, A5, 128 pages, *S/b £9.99*

**MERSEY SHIPPING, The Twilight Years,** by Ian Collard, A5, 128 pages, *S/b £9.99*

**BRISTOL CHANNEL SHIPPING – The Twilight Years**, by Chris Collard, (due October 2000) *S/b £9.99*

**SHIPWRECKS OF KENT** compiled by Anthony Lane A5 128 pages *S/b £9.99*

**BRUNEL'S SHIPS,** by Denis Griffiths, Andrew Lambert and Fred Walker, photographs, drawings and plans, 160 pages, *H/b £30.00*

**THE ALLIED CONVOY SYSTEM 1939 – 1945**, by Arnold Hague, 250 pages 280mm x 218mm, includes 46 photographs, *H/b £25.00*

**FERRY SERVICES OF THE LONDON, BRIGHTON & SOUTH COAST RAILWAY** by S Jordan, A5 format, 112 pages with over 110 photos, plans and illustrations, *S/b £8.95*

**RMS QUEEN MARY: Transatlantic Masterpiece** A5, 96 pages photographs including some in full colour, (due October 2000) *£14.99*

**ISLE OF WIGHT HERE WE COME,** The story of the Southern Railways Isle of Wight ships during the war 1939 – 1945 by Hugh J Compton. A5, 80 pages with 39 photos and plans, *S/b £6.95*

**RAILWAYS TO NEW HOLLAND and the HUMBER FERRIES** by A J Ludlam, A5  104 pages *S/b £8.95*

**SHAKESPEARE'S AVON**, The History of a Navigation by Dr Jamie Davies. Navigation on the River Avon which now forms part of the Avon Ring. Was the first steam ship built on this river? A5 152 pages with 98 photos and plans, *S/b £8.95*

**LINERS TO THE SUN**  (2nd edition) by John Maxtone-Graham, sequel to authors best seller The Only Way to Cross. Liners to the Sun which was first published in 1985. Chapters include building of ever larger cruise ships, history of the cruise business, famous cruises of the past, development and design of passenger cabins, life of stewards, cruise ships mishaps such as that of the *Prinsendam, QE2*'s boiler failure and *Rotterdam*'s encounter with a giant wave, modern cruising, *France/Norway, Fairsea, Sagafjord* and *Royal Viking Sea*, and smaller luxury ships. A vastly informative history of cruising and a jolly good read. 495 pages, 252 B&W illustrations. *Softback £19.95 or hardback £34.95.*

**OCEAN SHIPS 15th.Edt.** David Hornsby  *H/b £20.00*

**CRUISE SHIPS An Evolution in Design** by Philip Dawson *H/b £40.00*

*We though it was all sold out but it isn't:* **Duncan Haws – Merchants Fleets No.31 – ELDERS & FYFFES AND GEEST** *S/b £8.50*

**LINERS The Golden Age,** from the Hulton Getty Picture Collection by Robert Fox. Magnificent collection of photographs spread over 352 pages with captions and text in English, German and French, 302 x 266mm, *H/b £19.99*

**TANKERMAN** by Captain Dick Williams who served with Shell for 39 years. 247 pages  *£14.99*

**LANCASTER'S LITTLE SHIPS** – Robert Gardner's role in the Coastal Trade 1924-1962  by Edward Gray. Illustrated with fleet list, A5 40 pages *S/b £4.95*

**LANCASHIRE CANAL CARRIERS – J MONK & SONS**  by Norman Jones, James Monk Jnr and Leonard Monk.205 x 270mm 64 pages History of a company which traded on the canals of Lancashire. Well illustrated. *S/b £9.95*

**FULL LINE, FULL AWAY** Towboat Master's Story by James E "Ted" Wilson with S C Heal  Ted Wilson's career on Canadian tugs which started in 1933  152 x 228mm 168 pages, *S/b £9.50*

**TUGS BOOMS & BARGES** by R Sheret, Tugs and towage in British Columbia – types of tugs used, what they towed and life on the tugs. 215 x 278mm 124 pages with about 255 photos and 75 other illustrations *S/b £15.00*

**CONCEIVED IN WAR, BORN IN PEACE** Canada's Deep Sea Merchant Marine by S C Heal, ships built in Canada in both World Wars, 152 x 228mm 234 pages illustrated, *S/b £11.00*

**DIE DEUTSCHE SCHIFFSLISTE 2000** List of German Shipowners by Eckardt & Messtorff, Hamburg. 275mm wide x 142mm high, 200 pages 31 drawings 57 photos *S/b £23.50*

---

**THE WORLDS MERCHANT FLEET 1939** R Jordan Lists over 6000 ships which were afloat in 1939 and details the loss of the 3000 or so which did not survive the war. Includes over 300 photographs. **An excellent reference book and in our opinion one not to be missed.** *H/b £40.00*

**DIE DEUTSCHE HANDELSFLOTTE 1939** first published in 1953 this book, now reprinted by Eckardt & Messtorff, lists German merchant ships in service in 1939. 72 A5 pages of which the list takes up 13 and line drawings the remainder. Details of loss/later names given. *S/b £8.50*

---

*We now stock some books from Ferry Publications. Plenty of photographs, both colour and black and white and extremely well reproduced*

**IN FAIR WEATHER & FOUL – 30 years of Scottish passenger ships and ferries,** by Colin J Smith A4 128p *S/b £12.95*
**DESIGNING SHIPS FOR SEALINK** by Don Ripley & Tony Rogan A4 80p *S/b £8.95*
**GREEK FERRIES** by John May A4 112p *S/b £9.99*
**A CENTURY OF NORTH WEST EUROPEAN FERRIES 1900-2000** by Miles Cowsill & John Hendy, A4 192p *S/b £16.00*
**P&O THE FLEET** by Miles Cowsill, John Hendy & William Mayes, A5 96p *S/b £7.50*
**FERRIES OF THE BRITISH ISLES AND NORTHERN EUROPE** compiled by Nick Widdows, A5 224p *H/b £12.00*
**THE SEALINK YEARS 1970-1995** by Miles Cowsill & John Hendy 223 x 198mm 120p *S/b £9.95*
**P&O NORTH SEA FERRIES across three decades** by Barry Mitchell, 206 x 192mm 96p *S/b £6.95*

---

**ILLUSTRATED SHIP REGISTERS FOR YEAR 2000**
**DETLEFSEN'S ILLUSTRATED REGISTER OF GERMAN SHIPS 2000** 924 pages must be over 2000 pictures *S/b £32.50*
**DANISH ILLUSTRATED SHIP REGISTER 2000** *S/b £32.50*
**NORWEGIAN ILLUSTRATED SHIP REGISTER 2000** *S/b £35.00*
**SCHEEPVAART 2000** by G J de Boer. ( 24th edition of this well-known yearbook of Benelux shipping)  *S/b £17.00*
**SLEEP & DUWBOTEN 2000** by W van Heck and A M van Zanten (Dutch tugs, pushtugs, harbour tugs etc.) *S/b £16.00*
**BINNENVAART 2000** by W van Heck and A M van Zanten (Dutch inland waterways craft.) *S/b £17.00*
**DIE DEUTSCHE SCHIFFSLISTE 2000** List of German Shipowners by Eckardt & Messtorff, Hamburg. 275mm wide x 142mm high, 200 pages 31 drawings 57 photos *S/b £23.50*

---

**MISCELLANEOUS PUBLICATIONS:**
**ON A BROAD REACH – The history of the St Annes-on-Sea Lifeboat Station 1881-1925** by G.I. & J.E.Mayes *£12.50*
**GLORY DAYS TRANSATLANTIC LINERS** by David Williams 96pages 184 x 240mm 60 b&w photos 50 colour, *H/b £16.00*
**UNION FLEET** by Ian Farquhar fleet 1875/1999, 360 pages, 400 illus. (due November/December) *H/b price to be advised.*
**MALTA CONVOYS** by Richard Woodman *H/b £30.00*
**THE ELLAN VANNIN STORY** by Richard Stafford, lost Mersey Bar 1909, *£12.99*
**COASTAL SHIPS & FERRIES** David Hornsby *H/b £19.00*
**SEVERN TRADERS, The West Country Trows and Trowmen** Colin Green *H/b £26.95*
**SHIPS OF WELLINGTON** Victor H Young *H/b £14.50.*
**THE LOSS OF THE SS TREVEAL** by David Pushman. *S/b £7.95*
**THE SWANSEA COPPER BARQUES AND CAPE HORNERS** by Joanna Greenlaw *H/b £24.95*
**IRON CLIPPER 'TAYLEUR' THE WHITE STAR LINE'S FIRST 'TITANIC'** *S/b £7.50*
**UGANDA,** The story of a very special ship, The SS Uganda Trust, *H/b £25.00*
**IRONFIGHTERS, OUTFITTERS & BOWLER HATTERS** – G C O'Hara, Post war Clyde shipbuilding, 356 A4 pages *H/b £25.00*

---

**FROM PORTUGAL:**
**RMS QUEEN ELIZABETH 2** by Bill Miller and Luis Miguel Correia 100 pages full colour includes other Cunarders, English Text *S/b £12.00*
**SS CANBERRA of 1961** by Bill Miller and Luis Miguel Correia 68 pages full colour English text *S/b £9.00*
**SS ROTTERDAM of 1959** by Bill Miller and Luis Miguel Correia 68 pages full colour English text *S/b £9.00*
**LISBON DOCKS & SHIPS** by L M Correia pictorial book of Lisbon shipping 1975-96 96 pages in full colour *H/b £28.00*
**SOPONATA 1947 – 1997** by L M Correia company history and fleet list in English and Portuguese *H/b £35.00*

**HUTTON PRESS:**
**MARITIME FLEETWOOD** a photographic record, Alan Hirst and Peter Horsley, *S/b £12.50*
**HARRY HUDSON RODMELL** Shipping Posters and Graphic Works, Arthur G Credland *S/b £8.95*
**BOSTON DEEP SEA FISHERES** Mark Stopper and Ray Maltby *S/b £9.95*
**COOK, WELTON & GEMMELL** M Thompson  (a reference book not to be missed)  *S/b £16.95*

**TEMPUS PUBLISHING:**
**PADDLE STEAMERS OF THE THAMES** by Peter Box *S/b £10.99*
**P & A CAMPBELL PLEASURE STEAMERS 1887-1945** Chris Collard *£9.99*
**P & A CAMPBELL PLEASURE STEAMERS from 1945** Chris Collard *£9.99*
**THE WILSON LINE** Arthur G Credland *S/b £10.99*
**IMMINGHAM AND THE GREAT CENTRAL LEGACY** Ian Butler and Brian Mummery *S/b £9.99*

**MERCHANT FLEETS** by Duncan Haws (all softback)
- ❖  **38. FURNESS WITHY** Volume 2 *£21.00*
- ❖  **37. FURNESS WITHY** Volume 1 *£20.00*
- ❖  **36. MESSAGERIES MARITIME** *£14.50*
- ❖  **35. ROTTERDAM LLOYD** *£12.50*
- ❖  **34. LAMPORT & HOLT + BOOTH** *£14.50*
- ❖  **33. CLAN, HOUSTON, TURNBULL MARTIN, SCOTTISH TANKER** *£13.50*
- ❖  **32. UNION SS OF NZ.** *£14.50*
- ❖  **31. ELDERS & FYFFES AND GEEST** *£8.50*
- ❖  **30. FRENCH LINE** *£13.50*
- ❖  **29. HENDERSON & BIBBY** *£13.50*
- ❖  **28. HOLLAND AMERICA** *£11.00*
- ❖  **26. BRITAIN'S RAILWAYS: SCOTTISH & IRISH CO'S, MACBRAYNE + STENA** *£12.25*
- ❖  **25. BRITAIN'S RAILWAYS: NORTH WESTERN & EASTERN + ZEELAND + STENA** *£14.25*
- ❖  **24. BRITAIN'S RAILWAYS: WESTERN & SOUTHERN + FRENCH + STENA** *£14.25*
- ❖  **23. CANADIAN PACIFIC** *£13*
- ❖  **22. GLEN & SHIRE** *£8.50*
- ❖  **21. PORT, CORRY, ROYDEN, TYSER, MILBURN,** *£9.50*
- ❖  **20. ELDER DEMPSTER** *£15.00*
- ❖  **19. WHITE STAR** *£9.25*
- ❖  **18. UNION CASTLE** *£11.00*
- ❖  **17. ABERDEEN, ABERDEEN & C'WEATH** *£7.50*
- ❖  **11. BRITISH INDIA** *£12.00*
- ❖  **9. ANCHOR LINE** *£8.00*
- ❖  **5. ROYAL MAIL & NELSON** *£8.00*

**CARMANIA PRESS -** Excellent books with first class reproduction, Carmania often employ the same printer we use. Titles are self explanatory.
- ❖  **LAURENCE DUNN'S MEDITERRANEAN SHIPPING** by Laurence Dunn 132 pages *S/b £15.95*
- ❖  **THE NURSE FAMILY OF BRIDGEWATER AND THEIR SHIPS** by James Nurse. *S/b £5.95*
- ❖  **UNION-CASTLE LINE, A Fleet History** by Peter Newall. *H/b £32.00*
- ❖  **PASSENGER LINERS AMERICAN STYLE** by William H Miller *S/b £15.95*
- ❖  **THE SITMAR LINERS AND THE V SHIPS, 1928-1998** by Maurizio Eliseo, *H/b £26.00*
- ❖  **OCEAN LINER ODYSSEY, 1958-1969** by Theodore W.Scull *S/b £10.95*
- ❖  **GOING DUTCH - HOLLAND AMERICA LINE** *S/b £12.95*
- ❖  **LAURENCE DUNN'S THAMES SHIPPING** *S/b £12.95*
- ❖  **MERCHANT SHIPS OF A BYGONE ERA  -  THE POST-WAR YEARS**  *S/b £14.95*
- ❖  **THE COSTA LINERS** *S/b £12.95*
- ❖  **LINERS & CRUISE SHIPS (1) SOME NOTABLE SMALLER VESSELS** *S/b £12.95*
- ❖  **LINERS & CRUISE SHIPS (2) SOME MORE NOTABLE SMALLER VESSELS** Anthony Cooke *S/b £13.95*
- ❖  **NEW YORK SHIPPING** *S/b £11.95*

**BROWN, SON & FERGUSON LTD.** The fact that these books are still onsale, even if as reprints, so long after their original publication dates is testament to their quality, all by Basil Lubbock unless otherwise indicated:
- ♦  **THE CHINA CLIPPERS** *H/b: £22.00*
- ♦  **THE COLONIAL CLIPPERS** *H/b: £22.00*
- ♦  **THE LOG OF THE "CUTTY SARK"** *H/b: £24.00*
- ♦  **THE LAST OF THE WINDJAMMERS Volume 1** *H/b: £30.00*
- ♦  **THE LAST OF THE WINDJAMMERS Volume 2** *H/b: £30.00*
- ♦  **THE BLACKWALL FRIGATES** *H/b £22.00*
- ♦  **THE DOWNEASTERS** *H/b £22.00*
- ♦  **THE OPIUM CLIPPERS** *H/b £24 .00*
- ♦  **THE NITRATE CLIPPERS** *H/b £22.00*
- ♦  **THE ARCTIC WHALERS** *H/b £24.00*
- ♦  **COOLIE SHIPS & OIL SAILERS** *H/b £22.00*
- ♦  **WESTERN OCEAN PACKETS** *H/b £22.00*
- ♦  **ROUND THE HORN BEFORE THE MAST** *H/b £16.00*
- ♦  **BULLY HAYES-SOUTH SEA PIRATE** *H/b £29.50*
- ♦  **CRUISERS, CORSAIRS & SLAVERS** *H/b £35.00*
- ♦  **WEST HIGHLAND STEAMERS**  G E Langmuir *H/b £25.00*
- ♦  **CLYDE  RIVER & OTHER STEAMERS** Duckworth & Langmuir *Hb £25.00*

## WORLD SHIP SOCIETY publications:

- ❖ **THE ABERDEEN STEAM NAVIGATION CO LTD** by G Somner, 68 pages 20 photos A5 *S/b £8.50*
- ❖ **BRITISH EXPEDITIONERY FORCE SHIPS, BEFORE, AT AND AFTER DUNKIRK** by J de S Winser. *H/b £18.00*
- ❖ **WESTON SHIPPING** by Ken Garrett, *S/b £7.50*
- ❖ **WARSHIPS FOR EXPORT – ARMSTRONG WARSHIPS 1867 - 1927,** by Peter Brook. *S/b: £28.50*
- ❖ **MERSEY ROVERS** *H/b £33.00*
- ❖ **FURNESS WITHY** *H/b: £34.00*
- ❖ **COMBEN LONGSTAFF & CO.LTD.** *H/b £30.00*
- ❖ **SHORT SEA:LONG WAR,** *S/b £21.00*
- ❖ **CROSSED FLAGS,** *H/b £27.50*
- ❖ **WILH WILHELMSEN 1861-1994** *H/b: £24.00*
- ❖ **WILSON LINE** *H/b £24.00*
- ❖ **CAREBEKA 1939-1983** *H/b £30.00*
- ❖ **FRANK C STRICK & COMPANY** *S/b £15.00*
- ❖ **HADLEY (HADLEY SHIPPING CO.LTD)** *H/b £18.00*
- ❖ **CONVOY RESCUE SHIPS 1940-45** *S/b £12.00*
- ❖ **HAIN OF ST IVES** *S/b £8.50*
- ❖ **HAMBURG TUGS** *S/b £10.50*
- ❖ **DONALDSON LINE** *S/b £9.00*
- ❖ **H HOGARTH & SONS LTD** (1976) *S/b £3.50*
- ❖ **FROM 70 NORTH TO 70 SOUTH,** (Chr Salvesen 1984) *S/b £4.50*
- ❖ **GEORGE GIBSON & COMPANY** *S/b £5.50*
- ❖ **HISTORY OF SHIPBUILDING AT LYTHAM** *S/b £10.*
- ❖ **GORTHON SHIPPING CO. 1915-85** *S/b £4.50*
- ❖ **NORWEGIAN AMERICA LINE** *S/b £9.00*
- ❖ **THE NITRATE BOATS** *S/b £12.00*
- ❖ **DUNDEE PERTH & LONDON** *S/b £15.00*
- ❖ **DANNEBROG FLEET HISTORY** *H/b £39.00*
- ❖ **METAL INDUSTRIES** *S/b £12.00*
- ❖ **NOURSE LINE** *S/b £6.50*
- ❖ **THE TRADES INCREASE (Common Bros)** *S/b £15.00*
- ❖ **STAG LINE 1817 – 1983** *S/b £4.50*
- ❖ **LONDON & OVERSEAS 1948 – 92** *S/b £10.50*
- ❖ **WM SLOAN & CO LTD. 1825 – 1968** *S/b £3.00*
- ❖ **THE THISTLE BOATS (Albyn Line)** *S/b £5.50*
- ❖ **AUSTRALIAN NATIONAL LINE 1939-82** *S/b £5.50*
- ❖ **HEAD LINE 1877 - 1990** *S/b £9.00*
- ❖ **THE DEN LINE** *S/b £9.00*
- ❖ **THE GOLDEN CROSS LINE** *S/b £7.50*
- ❖ **TONY STARKE SERIES OF REGISTERS OF MERCHANT SHIPS** by Tony Starke & William Schell. (Temporarily not available until October/November) Years which will be available: **1890, 1891, 1892, 1893, 1894, 1900, 1901, 1912, 1913, 1914, 1915, 1916, 1917, 1918 (Vol.1), 1918 (Vol.2), 1919 Vol 1, 1919 Vol 2, 1949, 1950, 1951, 1952, 1953, 1954, 1955, 1959, 1976, 1977, 1982 and 1983.** *S/b in slide binders: £11.00 per volume.*

## WORLD SHIP SOCIETY PUBLICATIONS - new to our lists:

- ➢ **D.F.D.S.** *H/b £35.00*
- ➢ **CONVOYS TO RUSSIA 1941-1945** by Bob Reugg and Arnold Hague *S/b £13.50*
- ➢ **LEANDER CLASS FRIGATES** by Richard Osborne & David Sowden *S/b £15.00*
- ➢ **SLOOPS 1926-1946** by Arnold Hague *S/b £14.50*
- ➢ **THE TOWNS** by Arnold Hague *S/b £10.50*
- ➢ **THE "TYPE 35" TORPEDOBOATS OF THE KRIEGSMARINE** by M J Whitley *S/b £3.50*
- ➢ **FERRY MALTA** *S/b £4.00*
- ➢ **BLAND GIBRALTAR** *S/b £4.00*
- ➢ **CHAPMAN OF NEWCASTLE** (1985) *S/b £5.00*
- ➢ **THE CONSTANTINE GROUP** (1983) *S/b £4.50*
- ➢ **SCRAP AND BUILD** by D C E Burrell *S/b £5.50*
- ➢ **THE SAINT GEROGE STEAM PACKET COMPANY** by R H Greenwood and F W Hawks *S/b £4.00*

## FROM CANADA:

**HIGH SEAS – HIGH RISK,** Sudbury Tugs *H/b £16.00*
**A GREAT FLEET OF SHIPS/THE CANADIAN FORTS AND PARKS** by S.C.Heal, *H/b: £24.50*
**SMOKE ASH AND STEAM – WEST COAST STEAM ENGINES** by Robin E Sheret. *S/b £14.00*
**FULL LINE, FULL AWAY** A Towboat Master's Story by James E "Ted" Wilson with S C Heal Ted Wilson's career on Canadian tugs which started in 1933 152 x 228mm 168 pages, *S/b £9.50*
**TUGS BOOMS & BARGES** by R Sheret, Tugs and towage in British Columbia – types of tugs used, what they towed and life on the tugs. 215 x 278mm 124 pages with about 255 photos and 75 other illustrations *S/b £15.00*
**CONCEIVED IN WAR, BORN IN PEACE** Canada's Deep Sea Merchant Marine by S C Heal, ships built in Canada in both World Wars, 152 x 228mm 234 pages illustrated, *S/b £11.00*

## FACSIMILES OF PORT AUTHORITY HANDBOOKS, good reproductions, interesting reading, coal tipping rates 2d. per ton and much, much more.

**THE PORT TALBOT RAILWAY & DOCKS CO** *S/b £5.95*
**LYDNEY HARBOUR, DOCKS, AND CANAL** *S/b £3.95*
**DOCK DEVELOPMENTS AT NEWPORT,** about 1906 *S/b £4.95*

**DIE STINNES REEDEREIEN** *H/b £48.00*
**DEUTSCHEN SERIENFRACHTER** The two volumes describe the impressive number of 'series ships' built in Germany, from the famous wartime 'Hansa' A, B and C ships, through the post-war Liberty replacements and other standard designs.
❖ **Volume 1** *Hardback £28.00*
❖ **Volume 2** *Hardback £28.00*
**HAPAG LLOYD DIE ERSTEN 25 JAHE.** by Arnold Kludas. (Hapag Lloyd, the last 25 years), *H/b £28.00*
**REGISTER OF GERMAN COASTERS, CARGO AND CONTAINER SHIPS** by Gert Uwe Detlefsen, German Coasters, Cargo and Container Ships 500/1600 GRT to 5000 GRT from 1945-99. *H/b with slip in case £62.50*
**SCHIFFAHRT IM BILD/SHIPPING IN PICTURES - CARGO LINERS (1)** *H/b: £14.50*
**SCHIFFAHRT IM BILD/SHIPPING IN PICTURES – TRAMPS (1)** *H/b: £14.50*
**SCHIFFAHRT IM BILD/SHIPPING IN PICTURES – MOTOR COASTERS (1)** *H/b: £14.50*
**SCHIFFAHRT IM BILD/SHIPPING IN PICTURES – CONTAINER SHIPS (1)** *H/b: £14.50*
**SCHIFFAHRT IM BILD/SHIPPING IN PICTURES – CARGO LINERS (II)** *(due October) H/b £14.50*

**DEUTSCHE REEDEREIEN (German shipowners)** This is a monumental work with five main authors. Of a planned 20 - 25, 12 volumes have now been published. Each volume takes a number of German companies, large and small, gives a history of each and a fleet list, with extensive photographic coverage. Each 200 page A4 H/b includes over 300 photographs, facsimiles and maps, and is published in a limited numbered edition of 1100:

**Volume 1** Ernst Russ, Seereederei "Frigga", Bernh Howaldt, Gebr Petersen, Ragnar Nilsson, E Rickertsen, A Zachariassen.

**Volume 2** W. Bruns, Leer; Larsen-Reederei, Flensburg; Robert Müller, Hamburg; Tankreederei Julius Schindler, Hamburg; Schulte & Bruns, Emden/Bremen; Weidtmann & Ballin, Hamburg; Gebrüder Winter, Jork.

**Volume 3** Carl Robert Eckelmann, Hamburg; John T. Essberger, Hamburg; Johann Kahrs, Stade; Ewald Ottens, Cuxhaven; Friedrich & Manfred Preukschat, Danzig/Flensburg/Kiel; Reederei Richard Schröder, Rostock/Hamburg; Otto Wiggers, Rostock.

**Volume 5** Johann Haltermann, Hamburg; A. Kirsten, Hamburg; C. Mackprang, Flensburg; 'Nordstern'-Reederei, Hamburg; Reederei 'Nord' K.E. Oldendorff, Hamburg; F.G. Reinhold, Danzig/Hamburg.

**Volume 6** Baltisch-Amerikanische Petroleum-Import GmbH, Danzig; Helmut Bastian, Bremen; Esso Tankschiff-Reederei GmbH, Hamburg; M.A. Flint, Hamburg; A.F. Harmstorf & Co., Hamburg; Wilhelm A. Riedemann, Geestemünde/Hamburg; 'Trimar' Schiffahrts-Kontor GmbH, Hamburg.

**Volume 7** Johannes Ick, Danzig/Hamburg; Leonhardt & Blumberg, Hamburg; Matthies-Reederei, Hamburg; J.A. Reinecke, Hamburg; J.H.T. Schupp, Hamburg.

**Volume 8** H. Peters, Hamburg; JA Reinecke, Hamburg; Travemunde-Trelleborg Linie, Hamburg; Olau Line, Hamburg; Aquarius Seereederei Edgar Leicher, Hamburg; Reederei Hinrich Witt, Hamburg, Olhandels-& transport, Bremen.

**Volume 9** Leonhardt & Blimberg, Hamburg; Deutsche Shell Tanker GmbH, Hamburg; Washbay Line (Henry Stahl), Hamburg, Ernst Komrowski, Hamburg.

**Volume 10** B Richters, Rob Bornhofen, Deutsche Shell, Heinrich Schmidt, A Hansen, Heinrich Bischoff, Hermann Wulff,

**Volume 11** Union Partenreederei/Scipio & Co. (Reefers), Ernst Jacob, Flensburg, (cargo ships, bulkers, reefers and tankers), "Hedwigshutte", Heinrich Krohn of Travemunde, Rord Braren and H Reckmann.

**Volume 12** Johs Fritzen, Erich Drescher, Otto A Muller, Retzlaff Reederei, Hamburger Lloyd, Helfrid Fahje
*Each volume H/b £40.00*

**WAINE RESEARCH PUBLICATIONS** Most maritime enthusiasts will already be aware of Charles Waine's books, those who have not encountered them before are heartily recommended to add them to their library.
▪ **COASTAL AND SHORT SEA LINERS** *H/b £29.95*
▪ **BRITISH STEAM TUGS** *H/b £24.95*
▪ **STEAM COASTERS AND SHORT SEA TRADERS** *H/b £23.95*
▪ **THE STEAM COLLIER FLEETS** *H/b £24.95*
▪ **BRITISH OCEAN TRAMPS, Volume 1, Builders and Cargoes** *H/b £19.95*
▪ **BRITISH OCEAN TRAMPS, Volume 2, Owners and their Ships** *H/b £19.95*
▪ **OLD TIME STEAM COASTING** *H/b £16.95*
▪ **ESTUARY & RIVER FERRIES OF SOUTH WEST ENGLAND** *H/b £16.95*
▪ **BRITISH FIGUREHEAD AND SHIP CARVERS** *H/b £19.95*

**LLOYD'S OF LONDON PRESS LTD**
• **LLOYD'S WAR LOSSES – THE FIRST WORLD WAR** – casualties to shipping through enemy causes 1914-1918. *H/b £125.00*
• **LLOYD'S WAR LOSSES – THE SECOND WORLD WAR – Volume 1** – British, Allied and Neutral merchant vessels sunk or destroyed by war causes. *H/b £125.00*
• **LLOYD'S WAR LOSSES – THE SECOND WORLD WAR – Volume 2** – British, Allied and Neutral merchant vessels, Statistics – vessels posted at Lloyds as missing or untraced – vessels seriously damaged by war causes, British, Allied and Neutral warships and naval craft lost, vessels lost and damaged by mines or underwater explosions since cessation of hostilities, *H/b £125.00*